SITUATING MEDIEVAL INDIAN STATE

SITUATING MEDIEVAL INDIAN STATE

Edited by
R.L. Hangloo

COMMONWEALTH PUBLISHERS
NEW DELHI (INDIA)

SITUATING MEDIEVAL INDIAN STATE

EDITION 2024

ISBN 81-7169-322-9

Published by :
COMMONWEALTH PUBLISHERS (P) LTD.
4831/24, Govind Lane,
Ansari Road, Darya Ganj,
New Delhi - 110002
Ph. : 23272541, 23242541
e-mail : commonwealthpublishers2016@gmail.com

Distributed by :
ARJUN PUBLISHING HOUSE
4831/24, Govind Lane,
Ansari Road, Darya Ganj,
New Delhi - 110002
Ph. : 23272541, 23242541
e-mail : arjunbooks2001@gmail.com

Laser Typesetting by :
Dimple Computers
Delhi

Dedicated
to
Late Smt. Bhagwati Koul
for her secular views
and scientific temper

PREFACE

This book is intended to draw the attention of scholars, working on medieval Indian state from the over-emphasized generalisations to still neglected problems of regional specificities, the understanding of which would help to situate medieval Indian state better. With a perspective of this sort we would be in a position to analyse the actually existing state structures in order to assess how closely they approximate to already generalized categories, built upon the basis of an examination of historical processes. The degree to which this book achieves its purpose is open to question because that would further contribute to the growth of knowledge on the subject. For preparation of this volume I express deep debt to all contributors for their well-thought and meaningful papers. I would like in particular to thank Prof. Harbans Mukhia for his valuable comments and encouragement. I have been fortunate in having access to his perception and through understanding of medieval Indian economy and society. I must thank Prof. Irfan Habib for explaining to men in great detail the complexities of medieval Indian state during his brief stay at Shillong despite his many academic and other engagements. I also acknowledge sincerely the germane comments and encouragement provided to me by my friends Prof. V. Ramakrishna, Prof. G. Haragopal, Prof. M.I. Khan, Dr. Visier Sanyu, Dr. A. Murali and Dr. K. Lakshminarayana. I also thank Shri B.R. Verma for bringing out the volume in time. Lastly I thank my wife Sharika not because it is customary practice among scholars but for maintaining the family with serene and cheer amidst all those problems that stemmed from the turmoil in Kashmir partly because of the nature and working of Indian state.

Rattan Lal Hangloo

LIST OF CONTRIBUTORS

Jayanth Bhushan Bhattacharjee
Professor and Head, Deptt. of History,
North Eastern Hill University, Shillong, Meghalaya
Presently Vice-Chancellor, Assam University, Silchar

K.S. Mathew
Professor and Head, Deptt. of History,
University of Pondicherry, Pondicherry

R.L. Hangloo
Reader, Dept. of History
University of Hyderabad, Hyderabad, Andhra Pradesh

Chetan Singh
Reader, Dept. of History, Himachal Pradesh,
University, Shimla

I. Laxmi
Lecturer, Nizam College
Osmania University, Hyderabad

CONTENTS

Preface vii

List of Contributors xi

Introduction 1

1. Sayyids and the Shahmir State in Medieval Kashmir 1339-1470 A.D. 5
R.L. Hangloo

2. The Portuguese Trade and State in Sixteenth Century India 33
K.S. Mathew

3. The Mughal State in 17th Century Punjab 45
Chetan Singh

4. Formation of Dimasa State in Medieval North East India 71
J.B. Bhattacharjee

5. Nayankara System and the State in Medieval Telingana 120
I. Laxmi

Index 131

INTRODUCTION

ACCOUNTS of Medieval Indian state in various historical writings over past few decades constitute an immense literature, raising interesting questions and providing significant information for shaping the understanding of Medieval Indian state. The further study in this direction is necessitated by a host of questions, thrown up for historians by the problems of regional variations. Because it is the comprehensive understanding of regional history which would ultimately enable the historians to characterise the nature of Medieval Indian state. The broad concerns that arouse our intellectual curiosity on the subject are:

(a) What are the foundations of Medieval Indian state, did it have the structure and direction of its own.

(b) To what extent it followed its historical roots within India and how far the external influences shaped its character.

(c) Why did it behave the way it did in medieval centuries and to what extent it is responsible for determining the direction of various historical processes.

(d) How far the regional patterns contributed to the growth of overall medieval Indian design and what problems were generated by such a historical process in restricting or growing the general mode of social transformation.

The answer to all these questions can be provided by a detailed historical investigation into the whole complex of state dynamics touching not only the development and the phases of its transition but also its dialectical relationships to the economy and polity in various regions of its location. Because each region had its own peculiar societal format, political power structure, class configurations and other regional specificities in socio-economic and cultural patterns.

In retrospect the Medieval Indian state has passed through over-lapping historical circumstances and acted as a decisive solvent which constantly impinged on the socio-economic, political and religio-cultural life of Indian society as whole. The Turkish penetration pushed forward mightly the twin processes of growth of administrative institutions and economic integration with all its complexity. At the institutional level the medieval state began to grow as a dialectical consequence of the inter-play between the growth of long distance trade and resulting economic integration of medieval Indian social formation. The apparatus of state began to heavily depend on the appropriation of peasant production, privateering even the peasants means of production in the shape of various landed assignments. Though a part of the states income also came from internal and external trade which significantly contributed to the prosperity of medieval Indian ruling class, but unfortunately it was not aimed and directed at acquisition of money and its conversion into capital goods. Moreover bad and unsafe roads, the aridity of the climate of its some of the regions and the highly under developed infrastructure in general, were the additional factors that inhibited the transformation of forces of production. Besides the lavish consumption of political community consumed the tax revenues and trade incomes thus fettering the transformation of handicraft production into a higher form of socio-economic organization for more than expected period.

Although under Mughal rule particularly under Akbar's period the medieval Indian state profoundly attempted to establish the universal administrative machinery as a part of the process of strengthening its centralism and to accelerate the promotion of trade, agriculture and handicraft production but soon the internal disarticulation was let loose by various forces behind which the nobility of the mughal state stood distinctly. No efforts were decisively made to strove to subordinate such nobles to medieval states law which in course of time exacerbated acute social conflicts, growth of private power and heightened economic crisis. No wonder the medieval state was unable to provide any resistance to financial bankruptcy and political disintegration both at the centre and in its provinces.

In view of these circumstantiates what becomes necessary for scholars is to explore the nature of these forces and processes that sustained the medieval state for such long period at ideological and other levels and justified the very existence of such a state. Therefore an effort has to be made to identify the significant impressions left by the state on the dynamics of economic foundations or forces and religious experiences which went a long way to legitimize the functioning of Medieval Indian state. The institutional machinery of the state has to be understood as the means of state for execution of its authority and not the source. The question has to be examined whether it was the personal weakness of the rulers or their inaptness of polity that also led to the strengthening of the state from time to time. The reasons have to be sought for broad persistence of traditional beliefs, sentiments values and art forms maintained by the religious and other institutions to conserve the authority of the state.

Keeping in view all these problems the collection of essays in this volume, which deals with different periods and such widely scattered fields of inquiry, might even add confusion to the debate and seem falling short off expectations.

But, a collection like this becomes essential for its main purpose is to provide information and present facts under different perspectives for those historians who treat the characterization of medieval Indian state as the most significant and central to the study of medieval Indian state and society.

The discussion in this volume is provided in five main essays, each specifically devoted to a certain region and aspect of medieval Indian state. The comments and conclusions derived in all these essays are speculative and impressionistic because they are designed to offer only general historical situations. The absence of general conclusion is also intentional because this volume does not set out to say the last word about the Medieval Indian state but on the positive side the different perspectives on economic, societal, religious, and political aspects of state opened up by these essays allow a large room for the hope that the historical fraternity may exploit such studies for characterizing the nature of medieval Indian State.

1

SAYYIDS, AND THE SHAHMIR STATE IN MEDIEVAL KASHMIR
1339–1470 A.D.

R.L. Hangloo

WITH the onset of fourteenth century A.D., there appeared a general feeling among Kashmirees that the region of Kashmiri would register comparatively a peaceful era and the establishment of Sultanate would usher in an improvement in the conditions of people but after resuming the power Shahmir Sultans felt more concerned with the legitimation of their rule, treating the promotion of Islam and the patronization of Sayyids as more fundamental for perpetuation of their authority than any social transformation, affecting socio-economic conditions of people.[1]

1. Jonaraja; *Rajatarangini,* (Sanskrit), English translation by J.C. Dutt, 3 Vols., Calcutta, 1872, reprint 1990, Vol. III, pp. 15, 26-27. Mohammad Qasim Firishta; *Tarikh-i-Firishta,* (Persian), English translation by John Briggs under the title *History of the rise of Muhammadan power in India till the year 1612*, 4 volumes, 1829, Vol. IV, p. 389. Behind the voluntary acceptance of Islam by majority classes in Kashmir lay the expectation that the new rulers would overhaul the entire socio-economic and political system and respond to the immediate problems of people. But while claiming the loyality of their subjects the Shahmir Sultans were neither hostile to old political structure so far and so long it suited to them nor to the growth of new institutions which helped them in legitimation of their power. Therefore, Shahmir states negligence in completely mitigating the social injustice and poverty at lower ends of society was not unjustified. Because the ratification of their legitimacy was more important and central to Shahmir State, particularly when the administrative organisation and control were very insufficient to maintain the social order and to undertake steps for bettering the conditions of its subjects.

From the very beginning the Sultans of Shahmir dynasty (1339–1470 A.D.) felt that Islam was unquestionably a great issue in the establishment of Shahmir Sultanate in medieval Kashmir.[2] Because the conversions from Brahmanism to Islam were increasingly shifting the solidarity of various social groups from caste distinctions and other social disparities to their religious homogeneity.[3] In this entire process the Sayyids worked as religious missionaries, reciters of Quran and tradition, prayer leaders and sufis in *Khanqas* played a very sig-

---

2. It becomes very clear from the fact that all Shahmir Sultans except perhaps Zain-ul-Abidin (1420-1470 A.D.) thought that Islam was a secure political ideology for them and the law according to which they ruled. Sayyid Ali; *Tarikh-i-Kashmir,* Persian Ms. Research Department Library, Kashmir University, Srinagar. The author has an unpublished Urdu translation of the same, pp. 1-9. Firishta; *Op. Cit.,* p. 453, *Baharistan-i-Shahi* (anonymous), pp. 24-31. Infact all the persian chroniclers on Kashmir are replete with evidence to this effect. In the past the ideologies have been eliminated or set aside under the names of sects, heresies and religious errors. The hard and suggestive polemic between *Sunnis* and *Shias* is excellent example, of the ideological basis of the theological reason. Only modern critics of ideology can show that each orthodoxy is ultimately founded on Ideological postulate.
3. Sultan Shams-ud-din Shahmir (1339-1342 A.D.) realised that the role of Islam was a political necessity when the majority of subjects had accepted Islam as a popular religion the state needed to patronise it in order to complete itself as State. Besides the establishment of Sultanate did not only involve the doings in authority but also the response of those who were subjected. This necessitated the existence of Sayyids creating and maintaining the hierarchies of dominance and deference. Sayyid Ali; *Tarikh-i-Kashmir,* pp. 1-20. True that "the democratic state the real state does not need religion for the political completion, on the contrary it can disregard religion because the human basis of religion is realised in a secular manner". Karl Marx and F. Engels; (on Jewish question) collected works Vol. 3, Moscow 1975, p. 157, Mosonnenve, *Islam in Critique,* Larose 1984, pp. 34-44. But in some medieval societies with majority of subjects as muslims (as in case of Kashmir) the state recognised God as the supreme Governor at least in theory. H. Djait, '*Origins of Islamic state*', in *Islam state and society* edited by K. Ferdinand and M. Mozaffari (Studies on Asian topic), No. 12, London, 1988, pp. 74-82. In medieval Kashmir too Islam was an integral part of the state system and the protest against Sultan could be treated as protest against Islamic tradition and punished with law and the role of state enlarged and justified. For details see, Sayyid Ali; *Tarikh-i-Kashmir* and the description of *Baharistan-i-Shahi* on Sultanate period.

nificant role. Gradually their preaching and teaching encompassed all aspects of peoples life in medieval Kashmir and they took upon themselves the task of defining the nature of relations between the medieval state and society in Kashmir.[4]

They tended to emphasize that the newly constructed muslim community (*Umma*) was divine trust and the political power of Shahmir Sultans as a divine gift. In strengthening such ideas for legitimation of Shahmir Sultanate the Sayyids were also the beneficiaries of medieval stereotype being regarded by majority classes in Kashmir as spiritual, intelligent and learned. Consequently they emerged as the most influential group not only in religious matters but also dominated the political affairs of medieval state and in regulating the public order.[5]

To Shahmir Sultans (1339-1470 A.D.) the Sayyids appeared to be a self motivated and largely the prime movers in maintaining the social order and the authority of state of which they became an integral part in the process. While justifying the primacy of his claim to governance Sultan Shahmir (1339-1342 A.D.) felt that the promotion and application of Islamic tenets in the affairs of medieval state was an ideal way of deriving legitimacy to his rule. He tried

4. The interference of Sayyids in medieval Kashmir's polity is as old as Islam in Kashmir. Bulbul Shah was the first person to have enjoyed royal patronage under King Rinchana (1324-1339 A.D.) who accepted Islam. After him the Sayyids of *Suharwardi* order started dabling in the politics of Kashmir more actively. Hence from the very beginning there was a relationship of mutual dependence. The Sayyids build the mass base and helped the state in execution of its authority and the state maintained them with various grants. The Sultans solicited from Sayyids the formal legal acceptance of their politics in the form of the so called *Fatwas*. They included wide range of areas in society, economy and polity. Haider Malik; *Tarikh-i-Kashmir* (persian manuscript) Research department library Kashmir University, Srinagar, pp. 98-100. For details see Hassan bin Ali; *Tarikh-i-Kashmir* (Persian), folis 101ab. and *Tazkirat-ul-Shurna;* research department library, Kashmir University, Srinagar, (henceforth RDLKUS), pp. 112-113.
5. Mohibbul Hassan; *Kashmir under Sultans*, Srinagar 1967, pp. 47-70. G.M.D. Sufi; *Islamic Culture in Kashmir*, Delhi, 1979, pp. 48-116. This dominance reflected the Islamic orthodoxy as an official religion resulting from collaboration of the large number of Sayyids as *Ulama* with the medieval state in course of time.

to protect and promote the institution of *Umma* by preaching the *Hanfia* doctrines and created endowments for the upkeep of those who accomplished this task.[6] This popularisation of *Hanfia* doctrines at the hands of Sayyids, provided to him, an effective mechanism of acquiring a cultural unity and defence particularly when the beliefs in enumerable gods, deities and rituals were no longer in position to do so.[7] To further signify that the Shahmir Sultanate was a necessary consequence of spread of Islam in Kashmir Sultan Shams-ud-din Shahmir stuck coins and changed the *Laukika* calender by applying *Yazdgird* in the offices of medieval state.[8] He also ordered *Khutba* to be read in his name.[9] All these measures of Sultan clearly reveal his concern to harness the functioning of medieval state with the Islamic practices. Dossuki rightly remarks: "At the level of practice Islam functions as an ideology it is used in most cases consciously by a ruling class to legitimise its position justify its policies, create consensus, generate mass support and discredit opponents." In these endeavours the ruling class is highly supported to varying degrees by officials *Ulama* by *Sheikhs* and *Imam*.[10] It is true that

6. Firishta; *Tarikh-i-Firishta*, p. 453.
7. In fourteenth century Kashmir Shahmir dynasty did not claim the legitimacy by right of descent from the branch of *Khalifas*, therefore, the true basis of Shahmir rule was power as illustrated by the Sayyids who always stressed the authority of god as supreme and the *Charishma* of Sultan, the constitution of the community of solidarity which gave the Sultanate its cohesion, Sayyids Ali; *Tarikh-i-Kashmir*, pp. 1-33.
8. The new calendar was known as *Kashmiri Sanah*, Peer Hassan Shah; *Tarikh-i-Hassan* (persian), Urdu translation by Moulvi Ibrahim Vo. II, p. 151. Mohibbul Hassan says that the new calendar began with Rinchanas accession 1324 A.D. and conversion to Islam. According to him it was used in all official correspondence and later it was abandoned by Moughals. Mohibbul Hassan; *Kashmir under Sultans*, p. 46.
9. Firishta; *Tarikh-i-Firishta*, p. 453, Nizam-ud-din; *Tabquat-i-Akbari* (persian), English translation by B. Day and B. Prashad, Vols. 3, Calcutta, 1927, Vol. III, p. 638. See also J. Rodgeres, *'Coins of Sultans of Kashmir'*, *Journal of Asiatic society of Bengal*, Vol. LIV, 1885, p. 26.
10. A.E.H. Dossuki; *"the Islamic resurgence, sources Dynamics and implication"* in A.E.H. Dossuki, *Islamic resurgence in Arab world*, New York, 1982, pp. 17-18. This was the way Islam was used from above. From below Islam has been used as an instrument of opposition and change mostly by

(Contd. on next page)

in the beginning Sultan Shahmir tried to buttress the foundations of Shahmir Sultanate by befriending the important elements within the local nobility and sought their participation in the apparatus of medieval state in Kashmir. He initiated this process by marrying his own son to the local noble Lakshimakas daughter.[11] He also chose *Chaks* and *Magres* for manning the standing army.[12] The other measures of Sultan included the abolition of all oppressive taxes and reduction of land revenue to ⅙th of the total produce.[13] But all these measures appear to have been essentially motivated by political ends. Because by the time he took over as a Sultan of Kashmir the Sayyids were not so well entrenched in the Kashmiri society, therefore, Sultans dependence on such measures was the only source of achieving initial political stability. Otherwise the total silence over the existing tax structure etc., would have resulted in unprecedented political opposition to his rule. However, if Sultan Shams-ud-din would have been genuinely interested in improving the social conditions of people he would have initiated the fuller rationalisation of the revenue system and introduction of various institutions (for public welfare) similar to those of Sultan Zain-ul-Abidin (1420-70 A.D.) or Emperor Akbar in

---

(Contd. from previous page)

militant groups. They legitimize their opposition to existing state of things with reference to Islam. This part of Islamic revival can be interpreted as a response to crisis of legitimacy of ruling elites in many Muslim countries. In present case of Kashmir militancy can be defined a reaction to the failure of the elites in substituting secular ideas of legitimization for traditional Islamic legitimacy. To this crisis of legitimacy came crisis commanding immense social changes, unemployment and economic under development.

11. Jonaraja, *Rajatarangini*, Vol. III, pp. 26-27, Firista; *Tarikh-i-Firista*, p. 455. Nizam-ud-din Ahmad, *Tabqat*, Vol. III, p. 638.
12. Firista; *Op. Cit.*, pp. 453-455.
13. *Ibid.*, These measures should not be taken to imply a marked tendency towards secularisation of states nature because by then the state had not feed itself from the religious influence. Though these measures were tackled from a political stand point but that does not mean the state depended for its existence on welfare of people. In other words we can say that the state was also side by side with religion, again to justify its existence by developing a sense of responsibility which was abandoned after Sultan Shahmir.

Sixteenth century.[14] Similarly the standing army not only helped the state to demonstrate its power but also contained the growth of private power which would have otherwise been directed against the medieval state itself. In this regard one thing ought to be borne in mind that while considering *chaks* and *Magres* (the most important families of regions nobility) for raising his sanding army Sultan Shahmir took into account the dynamics of power relations of the twelfth and thirteenth century into account and therefore tried to exchange one controlling nobility against the other.[15] From the beginning of Shahmir rule these families of *Chaks* and *Magres* took on their own the fundamental role of structuring and restructuring the power relations till ultimately the *Chaks* established their political dominance.[16]

During Sultan Shahab-ud-din's reign (1353-73 A.D.) a large number of Sayyids entered in Kashmir as Sufis.[17] Most of these Sayyids migrated to Kashmir from various parts of central Asia not only because they were imbued with religious zeal but also for acquiring the opportunities of power, wealth and prestige thrown up by the Shahmir

---

14. N.K. Zutshi; *Sultan Zain-ul-Abidin*, pp. 91-114. Abul-Fazl; *Ain-i-Akbari* (Persian), English translation Blochman, Vols. 3, Calcutta, 1872-73 (Bib. Indica) until Shahmirs ascendency the Turkish migrants had played practically no part in the political affairs of the valley. With Shahmirs ascendency did they continue to remain perfectly contented with the traditional trade and other tasks or showed their interest in securing wealth and political career, can not be answered at the moment but that they would have been called upon to take the charge of an area and aid the advancement of Sultans authority, can not be disputed.
15. The Polity of pre-Sultanate Kashmir is replete with *role of Dammaras Ekangas and Tantrins* in power relations of state. It is most likely that Sultan Shahmir who served the pre-Sultanate state in Kashmir though only for short period in many capacities had fully understood the growing political aspirations of the *Chaks* and *Magres* and the ineffectiveness of others and therefore offered them important role in building his standing army.
16. Nizam-ud-din Ahmad; *Tabqat*, Vol. II, p. 619. See also Parmu; *History of Muslim in Kashmir*, Delhi, 1960, pp. 220-280.
17. Jonaraja, *Rajatarangini*, p. 26, Sayyid Ali; *Tarikh-i-Kashmir*, p. 1, Sayyid Ali has based his information on *Tarikh-i-Qazi Ibrahim* but other than him no one has referred to this persian chronicle in Kashmirs History.

Sultans in Kashmir[18]. Sultan Shihab-ud-din made all arrangements for rehabilitation of all those Sayyids who migrated to Kashmir during his reign. Perhaps thinking that they would give definite direction to medieval state in Kashmir in very curious and unexpected way. He granted large and fertile tracts of land for the maintenance of their establishments. Sayyids Hassan Simnani and Sayyid Haider were granted a number of villages in Kulgam *Pargana.*[19]

---

18. Mirza Hider; *Tarikh-i-Rashidi* English Translation by Sir E. Denison Ross with introduction by N. Elias, London, 1895, p. 432, Generally our Chroniclers have been more inclined to record the migration of Sayyids but how can one deny the fact that general discontent in central Asia and Persia during this period would not have displaced the members of officials classes, the families of nobles, merchants, peasants, craftsment and other who fled to Kashmir with their retainers and other members of establishment in search of sustenance. There are interesting anecdotes in our sources relating to migration of Sayyids to Kashmir. One author has attributed the migration of Sayyids Ali Hamadani to Kashmir to a dream in which Sayyid Ali was commanded to proceed to Kashmir for preaching of Islam. Zafar Badakishani; *Khulasat-ul-Manaqab* (unpublished Persian Manuscript), (Persian) RDLKUS, p. 573. Apart from the genuine problems existing in central Asia the Sayyids as Muslim missionaries seem to have been influenced by some other religion. The points of contact did exist between Christianity and Islam. But one cannot go that far. Because there is some uncertainty about influences and borrowings in early sufism or mysticism. The example of Christian monks and monasteries in the western part of Caliphate may well have impressed early Muslim sufis, but this could hardly be true of areas like Iran or Central Asia, when we do not find any evidence of early sufism in the west. Richard N. Frey; *The Golden Age of Persia,* London, 1975, p. 158. Perhaps what one needs to examine is the influence of Buddhism because the story of one of the early sufi Ibrahim-bin-Adham of Balakh (777 A.D.) is so much like that of Buddha that one wonders whether the biography of Ibrahim was fitted into pattern of Buddha. In fact all that is indicated by Ibrahim and his disciples shaqiq 810 A.D. of Bulk in the story Buddhist rather than Zorastrianism preached and practised them. On the basis of the evidence one can suggest that sufism in Iran and central Asia received as initial impulse from Buddhist monks perhaps on the famous *Naubahar,* Buddhist monastery or *vihara* in Balakh. Besides Shihab-ud-din Suharwardi 1234 A.D. founder of sufi order mentioned a group of people in Khurasan called *Shaguffia* who lived as ascetics in caves far from the towns. M.M. Sharif; *History of Muslim Philosophy,* Weisbaden, 1963, pp. 354.
19. Sayyid Ali; *Tarikh-i-Kashmir,* pp. 1-15.

Nagam Paragana was granted to Sayyid Taj-ud-din bin Sayyid Hassan.[20] He also opened a number of *Madrasas* where *Quran, Hadith* and *Fiqh* were taught.[21] During Sultan Qutub-ud-dins reign (1373-1389 A.D.) various families of Sayyids who entered Kashmir with their leader Sayyid Ali Hamadani in 1379 A.D. were also allotted lands.[22] Sayyid Jamul-ud-din Alai got chitar area in *Pargana* Khourpara[23]. Sayyids Firuz was allotted Sempora and its surrounding villages in *Pargana* vihi.[24] Sayyid Kamal got the entire area of Naidkhai.[25] Mir Sayyid Kazim was granted the area of lethpora.[26] *Pargana* olar was endowed to Mir Sayyid Rukum-ud-din and Mir Sayyid Fakhru-ud-din.[27] Sayyid Jamal-ud-din who was well versed in Islamic theology was made to stay in Srinagar for providing consultancy to Sultan and his subjects on necessary occasions.[28] Mir Sayyid Mohammad Qurashi and Mir Sayyid Mohammad Abdullah were also granted land and other facilities in Bijbehara.[29]

---

20. *Ibid.*, A large *Khanqah* was build at Shihab-ud-din pora in Srinagar which was maintained by the revenues derived from other lands in Nagam *Pargana.*
21. Aba Rafi-ud-din Ahmad; *Nawadirull-Albar* (Persian), RDLKUS, ff. 25-30.
22. Sayyid Ali; *Tarikh-i-Kashmir,* pp. 1-10.
23. *Ibid.*
24. *Ibid.*, The Sayyids as missionaries in these various areas would not have confined their activity solely to the preaching of Islam. Under the cloak of Islam the *Khanqah* popularised the persian writings, culture, traditions and other projects connected with social, economic and political organisation of Kashmiri society. They found that the religious fear was much more effective in country where feudal or ancient traditions were dominant. Therefore the Islamic form of punishments appeared to them quiet reasonable in controlling the feudal tendencies and in defending the social order.
25. *Ibid.*
26. *Ibid.*
27. *Ibid.*
28. *Ibid.*
29. See also G.M.D. Sufi; *Islamic culture,* pp. 37-38.
    Sufi says that these Sayyids established hermitages all over Kashmir which served as centres for propagation of their religion and by their influence definitely furthered the acceptance of Islam.

All these endowments to Sayyids and their *Khanqas* was also way of providing for their families. The Sayyids were fortunate enough to have these fertile zones for farming and they derived income from the voluntary labour of their disciples on these lands and also from the pious gifts of craft produce from peasants and artisans of their area.[30] Built on the brutal system of unpaid labour of their disciples the Sayyids accumulated large fortunes over a period of time in which religious and secular grants and the subjection of peasants and craftsmen defined the social system within the valley. These grants later enabled the Sayyids to designate their heirs as administrators in perpetuity with a fixed income. The Sayyids gradually adopted the local tradition at least with outward conformity to build the public character of their *Khanqas* and estates. Their endowments were free from the exactions of Shahmir Sultans and their officials.[31] Although the relationship on these estates can not be characterised as feudal in strict Western European sense but there were lots of constraints on the utilization of labour power of the peasants. The power of surplus extraction by Sayyids was aided by medieval state and the interests of people were subordinate to the states interest. The medieval state in Kashmir was feudal in the sense that it did primarily serve the cause of surplus extraction by religious and secular elements and also continued to forge the process of sub-infeudation.[32] The generosity of Shahmir Sultans in

30. *Ibid.*
31. Moin-ud-din Miskeen; *Tarikh-i-Kabir*, (Unpublished Persian Manuscript), RDLKUS, pp. 20-25.
32. *Ibid.*, See also Sayyid Ali; *Tarikh-i-Kashmir*, pp. 1-15. In European feudalism also the direct exploitation of monastic lands consolidated in compact granages practised by monks and converse made their estates more productive. Savings derived form this rational organisation or from their ascetic life could be used to extend and improve their patrimony. That is to say these monks by putting into practice the letter and spirit of rule unintentionally obtained a certain amount of surplus production. Trade developed as a necessary way of dealing with this surplus produce and this in turn provided further opportunity for territorial expansion. However, one consequence of this involuntary

(Contd. to next page)

looking after Sayyids won them the gratitude of Sayyids and an influential place in the over all Muslim community of Kashmir who held Sayyids in high esteem. However, this preferential treatment of Sayyids by sultans can not be attributed to their spiritual roles but it was the direct consequence of Sultans desire to consolidate the medieval state in Kashmir, and the resources to maintain their monopoly of power.[33]

The evidence on the relationship of religion and state in the medieval Kashmir is still incomplete but there is much to indicate that the relationship was based on many reasons, probably the most pre-dominant of them in practical sphere was that Islam and state must cooperate to protect and reinforce each other. In fact those who would like to know, how the two roles in polity (religious and Political) in the world of medieval Islam were brought into play in medieval processes of state formation, must start their investigation in earlier centuries. They must look back to understand the

---

(Contd. from previous page)

economic prosperity was a growing deviation from their original principles which led to transformation in religious quality of their monks life. Eventually they became landlords in receipt of rent like other seigneurial groups and at the same time declined economy. D. Knowles; *Monsatic order in England,* Cambridge, 1940, p. 349, see also L. Lekai; *'The White Monks', A History of the Cistercian Order,* Kachee, 1963, pp. 209-10 and 230.

33. All the Sultans were well aware of the importance of Islam in medieval Kashmiri society. Each of them diverted the influence of the religious establishments (Khanqas) towards their social and political goals and turned Islam into an instrument of states policy. The Sayyids provided in effect the Islamic legitimation for every act of Sultan with whom they were pleased. The Sultans like Shihab-ud-din (1355-1373 A.D.), Qutub-ud-din (1373-89 A.D.), Sikander (1318-1413 A.D.) further sought to cultivate their personal images as devoted muslims. It was under these Sultans that several of the migrant Sayyids the so-called spokesmen of religion found their way into the officers of state which were otherwise the preragatives of those who were part of secular inheritance of state. In return the Sultans received the general support from religious establishments occasionally when they intervened they found themselves in difficulties but such examples are rare. Hence Islam was closely connected with Sayyids compliance to ruling elite in Sultanate, Sayyid Ali; *Op. Cit.,* G.M.D. Sufi; *Islamic Culture,* pp. 32-69.

nature of functioning of Islam in terms of institutions and ideas which developed with the death of prophet the founder of Islam and persisted down to modern times.[34] Though the

34. The death of Mohammed on 8th June 632 A.D. produced great consternation among muslims of Madina, but Abubaker his most senior friend and leader of the community pacified them with these succinct lines, "if one worships Mohammed, died but if one worships God, is living and does not die and then to *Umma* he added, stretch forth thy hand that I may swear allegiance to thee". Richard J. Mecarthy; *The theology of Al-Ashari.* Beyroth, 1953, pp. 115-116. Muhammad's mission as a messenger of Allah had ended but his political, economic, social and religious leadership of *Umma* needed a replacement. A *Quranic* verse had already divinely sanctioned such a procedure which stated "oh *Ye* who believe, obey Allah, obey the messenger and those of you who are in authority and if *ye* have a dispute concerning in any matter refer it to Allah and messenger, if you are (in truth) believe in Allah and the last day that is better and more secure in the end". *Quran* IV 59. But soon Muslims were divided among themselves regarding the rules for the appointment of those in authority, however, the need for succession to Muhammed was never questioned while Ali, Mohammad's cousin and son-in-law prepared for the burial of his body, the prophet's *suhabs* (companions) hurridly convened a council in a roofed enclosure known as *Saqifa* of *Ban Saida.* A heated discussion ensured between the *Muhajurun* and the *Ansar* which led to the election of Abubakar as the successor. Abubaker thus became the *Khalifa* the successor of the massenger of God and in this way the *caliphate* was founded as an institution which had no equivalent and was destined never to have any outside the Muslim world. The caliphate lasted for centuries and many things were subsequently changed but the idea that the approval of *Caliph* was kind of contract imposing reciprocal obligation on the men elected and on his subjects gained ground and became a fundamental concept once the muslims had developed a juridical mentality. Laura vecia Vaglieri; '*The patriarchical and Ummayyads caliphates*' in *Cambridge History of Islam,* (Ed.) P.M. Holt, A.K.S. Lambeton, B. Lewes, Vols. 2, Cambridge, 1970, pp. 57-58. Infact the Sayyids of Shahmir Sultanate were not different than the *Ulama* of Delhi Sultanate "where the *Ulama* as a distinctive religious group, were exerting enormous influence on state craft because of importance they attached to *Quranic* law in matters of state craft. But it is interesting to note that this religious group was becoming too worldly in its Weltanschaung inspite of its too religious mindedness. The spirit of *Koranic* law which ought to guide them in their actual life as well as in matters of state was fast loosing hold on them. The *Ulama* were identifying themselves with the cooked ways of kingship and were justifying their chicanery of politics which could not be sanctioned by Islam" Ishwar Topa; *Politics in Pre-Mughal times,* Delhi, 1938, fn. 1., p. 94.

contribution of Islam in medieval centuries was very significant in the field of religion law, philosophy, science, art and literature but at the same time it must be remembered that the tradition handed down was not necessarily same for all parts of Islamic world.[35] Popular practices and beliefs varied with different social realities. In case of medieval Kashmir too the early Islam made the individual allegiance depend upon doctrinal legitimacy of the Sultan, not that the individual Sultan was possessed with any rights but because it was the *Quranic* requirement, if the Sultan wanted to demonstrate his faith in Islam. The efforts of Sayyids indirectly demanded the absolute obedience of people to Shahmir Sultans as a religious obligation defined in terms of *Shariat* and justified by *Quranic* obligation "obey God, Obey prophet and obey those with authority amongst you".[36] And it was this obligation which newly established Sultanate in Kashmir came to acknowledge as an essential element for maintenance of its authority. In course of time the relations between the Shahmir Sultans and Sayyids became very close and complex, based on mutual need but divergent interests. The Sultans needed legitimacy and the Sayyids the privileged position.[37] There developed many kinds of bonds between the

35. The Islamic conquerors brought a monotheism with them. They possessed force and value. This inheritance presented problems when rule on conquered lands in different regions had to be consolidated and regulated. The Ummayyads were able to rule for some time on the basis of traditional Kinship cohesion but such politics was far removed from original Islamic purposes, John A. Hall and C. John Ikenbery; *The State*, Canada, 1989, p. 31.
36. Quran; IV, p. 59.
37. For understanding how the ruling classes in a specific or particular region or a country rules, it becomes essential to discuss the nature of political and ideological structures. According to Antonio-Gramsci the dominance and Hegemony of a social class does not and can not solely depend on physical coercion. Ch. Monfee; *'Hegemony and ideology in Gramsci'* in Ch. Monfee Edited; *Gramsci and Marxist Theory*, London, 1980, pp. 168-204 for details see also C. Busci Glucksman; *Gramsci and the State*, London, 1980, pp. 47-48. However, the class domination rests on ideological consensus or general acceptance of primarily social

(Contd. to next page)

Sayyids and Sultans. Pledges of loyalty expressed in oath and the vows of gratitude for benefits received and hopes of future favours.

The Sayyids appear to have preferred in great majority to remain resident in rural areas where they rooted their establishments securely and also created social basis of the power of Sultanate. In urban areas too they developed into organisation and adopted to the conditions of urban life and derived special advantages through their continuous links with the powerful rural urban aristocracy.[38] Although the Sayyids differed racially in language, ethos and privilege from largely Kashmiri speaking people yet they took little less time to grow into various dominant orders such as *Suharwardiya, Qadri, Naqshbandi* etc. to exercise a paramount influence on social, economic, political and cultural life of medieval Kashmiri society.[39] The importance of the role and functions of Sayyids could scarcely be underestimated for the entire

---

(Contd. from previous page)

conditions. Therefore ideology has generally a very significant function in preserving the dominance. In case of medieval Kashmir although majority of the people had accepted Islam and there was little problem of religious heterogeneity but in terms of economic and social levels ideology had a significant role in integrating and converting the divisive tendencies. Therefore, Islam obtained a significant role when it was used as a means of legitimising existing social conditions. The Shahmir Sultans thought it fruitful to conceive Islam as an ideology. It is interesting that Islam as a political ideology has at least two functions. On one hand it could function as a stablishing force serving to maintain status quo and on the other serve as an agent of change and revolution. A.E.H. Dossuki; *Op. Cit.*, pp.111 and 271.

38. *Sayyid Ali; Tarikh-i-Kashmir*, pp. 9-23.
39. Only *Rishi order* was indigenously founded by Sheikh Nur-ud-din Rishi. See Daud Mishqati; *Asrar-ul-Abrar* (Persian), RDLKUS, f. 5a. See also for details Baba Nasib; *Rishi-nama*, RDLKUS. Sayyid Ali belonged to *Kubravi* order. Qazi Noorullah Shustri; *Majalis-ul-Mumminin* (Persian manuscript), RDLKUS, p. 286. Abdul Wahab; *Fatuhat-i-Kubravia, Nagshabandi* order was introduced in Kashmir during Sultan Sikanders reign (1389-1413 A.D.) by Sayyid Hilal. Mohammad Azam, *Tarikh-i-Azmi* (Persian), RDLKUS, p. 54. Sayed Niyamatullah Shah was the first to introduce Qadriya order in Kashmir, see Mohammad Hussain Qadri; *Fatuahat-i-Qadriya*, RDLKUS, f. 20a., see also Moin-ud-din Miskeen; *Tarikh-i-Kabir*, RDLKUS, p. 51.

Kashmiri society which was intensely stratified on social economic and religious basis before accepting Islam.[40] The Sayyids mitigated the divisive tendencies and tried to build up the frame work of common social and nomative order.

What one needs to emphasize here is that the emergence of Sayyids as a ruling elite of Kashmir was not only noted in multiplication of *Khanqas* but also in the above mentioned orders and their participation in functioning of medieval state.[41] The basis of these orders of Sayyids were various social groups for whom Sayyids acted as authoritative spokesmen of legal, social and religious matters. So diverse were the contacts of Sayyids that they played a crucial role in the process through which the social communication was carried on in integration of medieval Kashmiri society in a working whole.[42] These Sayyids led the people in prayers in mosques and other religious occasions and came to from a distinct stratum in medieval Kashmiri society. As a guardian of shared system of beliefs, values and practices, they were spread throughout the whole society, performing varied functions and attracting various degrees of public respect and allegiance.[43]

One of the prominent person Sayyid Ali Hamadani of *Suharwardia* order tried his best to set the pattern of his order, the members of which were allegedly prepared to die for their

40. Krishna Mohan, *A History of early medieval Kashmir*, Delhi, 1979, pp. V.N. Drabu; *Op. Cit.* By and large the deference in social rank was still preserved in a degree unimaginable in Islam and the co-existence of affluence and extreme poverty was more sharply contrasted. The power of medieval state was not made to aid the economic progress and surplus accumulation only but rather to serve the interest of enriching the politically powerful excessive consumption by Sayyids and spread of peasant wealth by them through political power.
41. Zutshi; *Op. Cit.*, pp. 15-16. It was under the influence of Sayyids that the Shahmir state subverted the Hindu customs, they were also denied the official positions and music was banned totally in the kingdom. *Baharinstan-i-Shahi*, pp. 24, 31, Jonaraja; *Op. Cit.*, pp. Abdul Waheb; *Op. Cit.*, f. 157b. However, all these measures had political reasons not religious.
42. Moin-ud-din Miskeen; *Tarikh-i-Kabir*, pp. 12-28.
43. G.M.D. Sufi; *Islamic Culture*, pp. 32-47.

convictions and marvelously opened the way for application of Islamic tenets in the offices of medieval state under Shahmir Sultans.[44] He spared no trouble in asserting the position of the other members of his order and in justifying their necessity in all spheres of peoples life by seeking recourse to Islamic precedent and *Shariat*.[45] Parmu observes, "the Sayyid Ali Hamadani and his devote band of musalman disciples, the social and religious lie of Kashmir was an anathema and an abomination as it militated against Islam that was preached and practised in the name of prophet and pious *Khalifas*. They were too anxious to free Muslims of Kashmir from Hindu incrustrations. Therefore, Sayyid Ali took upon himself the task of transforming Kashmir. He first preached true Islam, preached and practised by prophet to Sultan Qutub-ud-din, both by precept and example. He influenced him with his spiritual powers which he possessed in abundance. His sway over the mind of Sutan was complete. When at his instance his unislamic marriage is annulled. One

---

44. Sayyid Ali; *Op. Cit.*, pp. 3-10, Mirza Haider; *Tarikh-i-Rashidi*, p. 432. For the establishment of Shahmir Sultanate Islam served as an ideology. The ideas about state, government laws regulating economic life moral and ethical norms, jurisprudence, as believers behaviour and the entire mode of life of the Muslim community was based on Islam. However, it does not necessarily mean that medieval state in Kashmir was an Islamic state. The specificity of Islamic state is the existence of a special systems of organs and institutions which fulfilled the functions of the state, power and law and which consolidates a judicial system of norms, sanctioned by Islam and for promotion of Islam purely for religious reasons Gusyam Mamed Ogly Kerimov; *'The Socio political aspects of modern Islamic mission'* (edited) in K. Ferdinand and Mehadi Mozaffari; *Islam, state and society*, London, 1988, pp. 44-45. In case of Kashmir the promotion and patronization of Islam took place for it provided an effective political ideology, therefore, the promotion of Islam was not solely for religious purposes.
45. Sayyid Ali; *Tarikh-i-Kashmir*, pp. 1-16. Sayyid Ali Hamadani expected *Amma-i-Khalaq* (majority classes) to strictly obey the laws prescribed by *Asharite* system of *sunni* theology, Sayyid Ali Hamadani; *Zakhirat-ul-mulk* (persian), RDLKUS, pp. 6-7. *Shariat* had grown up by a slow and complicated process of interaction between the norms contained in the *Quran*, *Hadith*, the local customs and laws of communities brought under the rule of Islam. So there was a continuous process of mutual adjustment between *Shariat* once it took its definite form and practice in muslim society.

of the two Sisters was taken into wedlock after performance of *Nikah* (marriage) while the other was divorced for ever. He also induced the Sultan to adopt muslim style of dress and introduce it among muslims subjects. Then he collected important rules of *Shariat* for guidance of Sultan and his muslim subjects and appointed his most truthful disciples as his religious mentor. Then he made a gift of his *Kulahi Mubarak* (cap or head gear) to Sultan and blessed his progeny with long life".[46]

From this account it becomes clear that the interference of Sayyids in the affairs of medieval state under Sultan Qutub-ud-din had come more than half way. Now the issue was not only of the application of Islamic tenets in the affairs of state but it reflects the efforts of Sayyids to control and direct the affairs of medieval state for their personal political ends. They gradually began to emblish Sultans court, gave him the reputation for munifience and in return tried to obtain official positions in civil and judicial administration.[47] They existed above all the promote the interests of their own members through political competition and their first unifying political principle was the prospect of the material awards of land and offices of medieval state for their various roles. They were although concerned with mass following, although their reason for doing so evolved over a period of

46. R.K. Parmu: *A History of Muslims rule Kashmir*, pp. 105-106 for details see Muhammad Azam; *Tarikh-i-Azami*, p. 30. G.M.D. Sufi says that Sultan Qutub-ud-din had such a great regard for the cap given to him by Sayyid Ali Hamadani that he always wore it under his crown. The cap was passed on to succeeding Sultans and was finally burried with the dead body of Sultan Fath Shah in 1517 A.D. According to Sufi someone prophesied that the burial of the cap would be an indication of the end of the dynasty. It is curious co-incidence that the Shahmir dynasty came to an end around the same time. G.M.D. Sufi; *Islamic culture in Kashmir*, p. 38. Such an approach has generated a wide range of question which are central to the study of political history. In fact they centre around the functional relationship between power and mystical phenomenon, which makes the notion of power eventually problematic because some times historian tends to treat subject of ceremonial as fundamental while reconstructing history.
47. *Baharistan-i-Shahi*, pp. 29-30. There are plentiful references to show that Sayyids acted in various capacities in secular jurisdiction of the *Sultanat*.

time because the Sayyids who sought to win the peoples support or could claim their allegiance in any particular area, were in good position to claim a corresponding prominence at Sultan court.[48]

Under Sultan Qutub-ud-din (1373-89 A.D.) the medieval state made a weighty advance towards the assimilation of Sayyids as the political ideologues which resulted in delimiting the accesses of non-Sayyids nobility in the affairs of medieval state in the long run.[49]

With the Sultan Sikander (1389-1413 A.D.) a period of permanent interaction commenced between Kashmirees and people of central Asia. Many more Sayyids entered the valley with their leader Mir Mohammad Hamadani, a brass tongued preacher Sayyid Mir Mohammad was accompanied by three hundred Sayyids when he arrived in Kashmir in 1393 A.D.[50] Like his predecessors Sultan Sikander granted lands and made all necessary arrangements to settle them in various parts of the valley. The *Khanqah* of Mir Mohammad Hamadani in Alaud-din Pora in the heart of Srinagar was endowed various villages by Sultan Sikander to provide subsistence to its inmates and for other expenses.[51] Sultan Sikander's reign marked an era of very active participation of Sayyids in medieval state which was not discerned until then on such a large scale. Sultan Sikander created post of *Sheikh-ul-Islam* to head the department of eclesiastical affairs, judiciary and

---

48. They include Mir Sayyid Haider, Sayyid Jamal-ud-din, Sayyid Kamal, Sayyid Kamal Isfahani, Sayyid Jamal-ud-din Alai, Sayyid Feroz alias Sayyid Jalal, Mulla Ahmad Allami, Sayyid Ali Hamadani, Sayyid Azizulah, Mir Mohd. Hamadani, Sayyid Jalal-ud-din of Bokhara popularly known Makkodum Jehan, Sheikh Rukun-ud-din Alam, Sayyid Taj-ud-din, (cousin of Mir Sayyid Ali Hamadani, Sayyid Masud, Sayyid Yousuf, Sayyid Hussain Simnani, Sayyid Ali, Sayyid Ahmed Isfahani, Sayyid Mohammed Khawarzimi, Moulana Mohd. Sajad, Baba Haji Adham of Bokhara, Baba Hassan of Balakh, *Ibid.*, p. 34.
49. *Ibid.*, p. 29. See also Sayyid Ali, *Op. Cit.*, pp. 8-10.
50. Sayyid Ali; *Tarikh-i-Kashmir*, pp. 1-7, 25, 29. It seems the Sayyid Ali Hamadani and his son Mir Mohammad Hamadani 1339 alone brought into Kashmir more than one thousand of Sayyids to popularise Islam Sufi; *Op. Cit.*, pp. 38.
51. *Bharistan-i-Shahi*, pp. 29-31, Sayyid Ali; *Op. Cit.*, pp. 10-12.

offered this to Sayyids to enforce *Shariat* on the Hindu converts in medieval Kashmir.[52] *Shariat* the divinely revealed law of God had absolute authority. It preceded the state and was its law but there was no question of this law embodying the consent of those whom it was applied.[53] The subjects of Shahmir state had no right against the medieval state but only the expectation that the Sultan would at least act in confirmity with the newly established law in Kashmir. The combining of the post of *Sheikh-ul-Islam* with the judicial administration had very significant political overtones. The application of muslim judicial law was arrived at critical notions of legal equality in the eyes of Islamic law and this would have helped to attract more and more people towards Islam and indeed towards new political system. Therefore, concentration of judicial powers in the hands of *Sheikh-ul-Islam* was considered an important instrument in hegemonising the population and is strengthening the centralising spirit of states authority.

It seems that Sultan Sikander was unfortunately under the impression that a true Sultan was what he was not by the will of his own but by the grace of Sayyids who would open up great potentialities in public for consent to his rulership. He also believed that the execution of authority by Sayyids would play a great role in future growth and perpetuation of his sovereignty. Because in public eyes the extension of the authority of Sayyids in the functions of medieval state was seen as the fulfilment of divine precepts.[54] The Sayyids did

52. *Ibid.*, p. 31.
53. The *Shariat* has grown a long way in maintaining the unity to *Umma* in its ethical and religious attitudes. It was therefore considered the principal duty by Muslim government of Sultans to enforce obedience to *Shariat*. Besides the duties performed by muslims in fulfilment of laws of *Shariat* were not invalidated. Ibn-ul-Bazaz; *Al-Kadariya*, Hyderabad, 1903, pp. 15-16.
54. *Baharistan-i-Shahir*, pp. 23-24. His encouragement to Muslim and learned men attracted to his court a large number of missionaries and scholars from Persia and central Asian countries. They came in groups the most important one was of 300 Sayyids and scholars led by Sayyid Mohammed Hamadani, the son of Sayyid Ali Hamadani, soon they occupied the highest offices of the state. The Sultan came under the spell of Sayyid Mohammad and became his disciple in word and deed. The

(Contd. to next page)

not admit the existence of medieval state under Shahmir Sultans as an organisation in its own right but emphasised that the promotion and patronization of the process of Islamization by whatever means was a necessary component for the extension of the authority of Sultan in medieval Kashmiri society. They made him to validate his claim to sovereignty by faithfully depending on their advice while dealing with the affairs in medieval state.[55] Sultan Sikander perhaps felt that Islam was the only basis of political unity and it was the spread of Islam at the hands of Sayyids that constituted the main claims to legitimacy and loyalty of his subjects. This underlines the fact that the stability of medieval state in Kashmir was tied up with Islam as the right religion and its acceptance by majority classes. For spreading of Islam the Sayyid migrants kept on penetrating wider rural and urban society.[56] It was in this process that the large sections of rural poor owed allegiance to them for having controlled their social and economic life. Particularly when Sayyids retained the control of large proportions of cultivable waste in areas like Vihi, Nagam, Sempora, Tral, Nunwani, Chitar, Avanmpora, Naidkhai, Mortand, Bijbehara, Khourpara, Lar, Pakh, Vachi, Soura, Kulgam, Biru, and various other areas.[57] The Sayyids gained unlimited and unrestricted accesses to power of medieval state. They dominated all fields of human society and developed into a landed aristocracy within the medieval Kashmiri society. Reinforcing the close relationship between their order and various classes of society was strong current of social mobility and the entry into the body of Sayyids was formed by values implicit in muslim notions of status, wealth and respect, almost universally available to

---

(Contd. from previous page)

Sayyids resolved to dispel the darkness of infidelity from kingdom and shaped the Sultans attitude towards non-muslims. Abdul Wahab; *Op. Cit.*, p. 25, 29, 33.

55. Parmu; *Op. Cit.*, p. 117. Haider Malik, *Tarikh-i-Kashmir*, p. 29. See also Percy Sykes; *History of Persia*, Vol. II, pp. 130-34, Parmu observes "The Young Sultans associates and advisers consisted mainly Baihaqi Sayyids who had left their home in Subzwar led by Sayyid Mohd. Baihaqi, after being defeated by Timmur."
56. Sayyid Ali; *Tarikh-i-Kashmir*, pp. 1-20. Sufi; *Islamic culture in Kashmir*, p. 37.

them with the royal patronage of Shahmir Sultans.[58] The extension of their influence into the secular areas of States functioning also helped them to develop at best fairly effective coordination of action in their localities and provided basis for selective orderly allocation of geographical spheres of political influence. Their influence into administration was constant. No official, even if he desired, to fulfill his administrative duties while standing aside from political intrigue rapidly discovered that this was impossible either he had to resign himself to official inactivity or to act according to the instructions of Sayyids, to preserve his official position.[59]

At the rural level also they over shadowed the non-Sayyid nobles, although both derived their strength from the village extractions yet the non-Sayyid nobles fell to them (Sayyids) for they had assumed more extensive and arbitrary powers in settling of disputes, divorces, punishments and the presiding over various socio-religious occasions as local *Qazi, Mufti* or *Imams* for being well versed in Muslim theology though at times unfamiliar with local traditions.[60] Besides the complete

57. Sayyid Ali; *Op. Cit.*, pp. 3-17.
58. Haji Mohi-ud-din Miskeen; *Tarikh-i-Kabir*, pp. 21-25. All the Sultans extended their patronage to them during Shahmir Sultanate.
59. The conversion of chief minister Suhabhata during Sultan Sikanders reign is one of interesting example in this regard. *Baharistan-i-Shahi*, p. 24. See also Malik Safi-ud-din (Suhabhata) held very important position at the court of Sultan Sikander and Sultan Ali Shah (1413-1419 A.D.) yet he only carried out what the Sayyids wanted. He had to follow their instructions at every step very strictly. Jonaraja; *Op. Cit.*, p. 60.
60. *Qazi* had a certain competence in penal matters and regarding certain acts which were specifically prohibited by *Quran* and to which precise penalties were attached like unlawful sexual intercourse and theft. He also had more general authority to punish acts which offended against religion. Infact most criminal justice particularly in regard to matters which torched the welfare of *Sultanate* were administered by Sultan or his officials and not by *Qazi* (e.g.). The administration of justice which was generally left to *Qazi* the law was not so flexible as might appear from law books. The *Qazi* mostly seems to have interpreted his role as conciliator attempting to preserve social harmony by reaching on agreed solution to a dispute rather than applying law strictly. However, the Sayyid as *Qazi* was a central figure in the life of a city or *Pargana* because he not only administered law but was also responsible for division of property after persons death in accordance with the medieval Kashmiri laws of inheritance and had the power of supervision given to him by Sultan, Zutshi; Zain-ul-Abidin, p. 121.

networks of inter family relations among Sayyids, also provided a readymade machinery for arbitration of disputes which would have otherwise been referred to the court of Shahmir Sultans.[61]

Interestingly whenever the Sayyids worked for Sultans they immediately posed to exact a price for their cooperation in such enterprises and often used the occasion to increase their own power, wealth and prestige. The assistance on all such occasions was solicited by Sultan not sought by pre-empty order.

Under Sultan Sikander the Sayyids sought a clear mandate from Sultan to deal with all decisions. Their overriding influence led to series of civil strifes which the Sultan was forced to put down with strong hand.[62]

Therefore we are apt to think of Sultan Sikanders reign as one of interesting and critical periods in the history of medieval state in Kashmir. For he (Sultan) stroked up all chords of duties incumbent upon him as Sultan even though his contemporary Chronicles pandit Jonaraja does not dwell objectively or with critical appreciation on his reign. The iconoclast fury of Sultan Sikander seems to have shocked him more than anything else in the Kingdom.[63] Basically the Chronicler has failed to notice the ideological significance of Sultan Sikanders measures and therefore it deserves an observation.

Sultan Sikanders reign should not appear startling for he was only vigorously trying to establish firm foundations of

---

61. Jonaraja; *Rajatarangini*, Vol. III, p. 60. Mir Mohd. Hamadani was married to daughter of Malik Saif-ud-din a Hindu convert. Hassan Shah the son of Sultan Hider Shah (1470-72 A.D.) was married to Sayyid Mirak Hassan Baihaqi's daughter. Srivara; *Op. Cit.*, pp. 184-185. See also Nizam-ud-din, *Tabqat*, Vol. III, p. 446. Besides the exemption and enforcement of Islamic law would not have been possible without the appointment of Sayyid as *Qazis* and *Muftis*. Sayyids Hassan Shirazi was the *Qazi* of Sultan Sikander, Mir Mohd. Hamadani was the *Sheikh-ul-Islam* of Sultan Sikander.
62. Jonaraja; *Rajatarangini*, Lieut. Col. Newell, *'A sketch of Muhammeden History of Kashmir'*, JASB, 1854, No. 5, p. 415.
63. Jonaraja; *Op. Cit.*, p. 60.

the Shahmiri State with the help of Sayyids. The persecution of some of the Hindus and the destruction of some of their religious establishments under the instructions of Sayyids high lights the inter-dependence of religion i.e., Islam and the state. For if the right religion (Islam) helped to generate the political stability for Shahmir Sultanate it also needed a coercive arm to enforce where persuasion did not work.[64]

However, it was in this process that the offices of medieval state incurred the dangers by the Sultans submission to Sayyids. Zutshi very rightly remarks "in the sweep of his religious enthusiasm enforced by exhortations of religious fanatics, Sikander was carried off his balance and committed excesses against non-Muslim subjects. The result was a wide spread confusion in their ranks. The confusion became worst confounded under Ali Shah (1413-1419 A.D.) who while perpetuating the atrocities in a greater magnitude failed to stereotype the restructured government after the Islamic fashion, for he was a weak and inefficient ruler".[65] The Sayyids managed their religious roles with political control and socio-economic monopolies. Though they saw themselves as proud and dignified but in actual practice they were impious and extortionists. By the end of Sultan Sikander reign the Sayyids had become so much powerful that they dominated both secular and religious jurisdictions of medieval Kashmiri state and society, so as to occupy something of a politico-cultural hegemony. Their ambition soon found expression in political terms, primarily in competing alliances each of which draw its recruits from several social levels of power, prestige and wealth to directly transfer political power in their own hands.[66]

---

64. As a ruler Sultan Sikander was able and generous. He abolished many oppressive taxes, like *Baj* and *Tamgah*. He is also said to have established schools and hospitals. He banned the use of wine and other intoxicants, prohibited gambling and also abolished *Jazia*. This clearly indicates that he was interested in Kashmir's affairs. *Baharistan-i-Shahi*, pp. 30-36.
65. Zutshi; *Zain-ul-Abidin*, p. 93.
66. Abdul Waheb; *Op. Cit.*, f. 156a, *Baharistan-i-Shahi*, pp. 29-30, Sayyid Ali; *Op. Cit.*, pp. 9-15.

They found a very suitable opportunity in the reign of Sultan Ali Shah (1413-1419 A.D.). They joined their hands with Sultans prime minister Saifu-ud-din, a Hindu convert, in a scheme to extract taxes and to coerce subjects of Shahmir Sultans.[67] Sultan Ali Shah became totally ineffective when the Sayyids were led by Mir Qaiser in directing the apparatus of medieval state for their personal ends.[68] They threw Kashmir in the state of confusion by violating the wives of Kashmirees, subjecting them to inequalities exactions to all sorts of oppression even the Sultans property was not spared.[69] Jonaraja says "Lofty homes, excellent houses, fine dresses, large gems and all that adorned the king (Ali Shah) were now rested by a yavanas (foreign Muslims)".[70]

With this articulated emergence of Sayyids as ruling elite the other non-Sayyid elements within the local nobility found their interests curtailed their positions challenged and their power threatened. The rise and domination of Sayyids was seen by them as their political enemy and the doting of multiple *Khanqas* on the surface of Kashmir as the power centres to be manipulated in order to stage direct political ascendency.[71] The non-Sayyids nobility was not easily satisfied with being relegated to important albeit prestigious political oblivion. Both the Sayyids and non-Sayyids nobility had definable

67. Infact Malik Saifuddin was the active supporter of Sayyids who tried to assume more and more power when he found that Sultan Ali Shah was ineffective. It was at this time the non-Sayyid nobles like Ladi magre found their power in the affairs of the state was restricted and rebelled against the designs of Mallik Saifuddin. Jonaraja; *Op. Cit.*, p. 61, Firishta, *Tarikh-i-Firishta*, pp. 467-68.
68. N.K. Zutshi; *Op. Cit.*, p. 35.
69. *Ibid.* See also Jonaraja; *Op. Cit.*, p. 73.
70. *Ibid.*
71. In fact the non-Sayyid nobility does seem to have protested from the very beginning of Sultanate when they found that the Sayyids were assuming more and more powers. For example the rebellion of Lakshman Bhat during Sultan Jamsheds reign (1342-1343 A.D.) and the revolt of *lavanyas* under Sultan Ala-ud-din (1343-1354 A.D.) should not be treated as isolated incidents. M. Hassan; *Op. Cit.*, pp. 47-48. After the death of Hassan Shah (1472-84 A.D.) the Baihqi Sayyids directly controlled the power of state in 1519, Jonaraja; *Op. Cit.*, pp. 65-70.

political goals which set them at odds with the medieval Kashmiri state. With the increasing power of Sayyids the state was proportionately weakened and therefore, not only did the Sultan Ali Shah's ability to control the situation decline but also did his ability to rule.[72] As a result the factional rivalry within the medieval Kashmiri nobility tended to increase, weakening the state further and rendered Sultan Ali Shah merely *primes interpares* among institutions of medieval Kashmiri society. But the crisis at this stage were halted though only for a while by the succession of Shahi Khan popularly known as Sultan Zain-ul-Abidin (1420-1470 A.D.).[73] In his efforts to strengthen his claims to capture power Zain-ul-Abdin depended on non-Sayyids nobility. He entered into an alliance with *Thakurs* and other local chiefs of southern Kashmir to rest power from rival claimant Yousuf Khan who was defeated and killed in 1418 A.D. at *Idgah* in Srinagar.[74] Out of these chaotic conditions Sultan Zain-ul-Abidin tried to shape strong and coherent traditions to strengthen the bare elements of medieval state. Under him medieval state settled itself and found itself as it had never done before. Sultan Zain-ul-Abidin scrupulously avoided grabbing of dictatorial powers by Sayyids at his court.

He did not hesitate in expelling Sayyid Mak, when the

72. It was clearly as a result of discontent and factional fights among the local nobles that made Ali Shah to abdicate in favour of his son Shahi Khan who later adopted a soft attitude towards the non-Sayyids nobles. The *Thakurs* who supported his claims were the band of local nobility. M. Hassan, *Op. Cit.*, pp. 67-70.
73. Jonaraja; *Op. Cit.*, pp. 75-97. Firishta; *Op. Cit.*, p. 468. Zutshi rightly says, "His (Ali Shahs) decision to abdicate in favour of his son Shahi Khan was indeed, the outcome of his utter indifference to manage the state, the political affairs of which" had gone against him to the extent that he preferred going on pilgrimage to being dethroned by Shahi Khan". Zutshi; *Op. Cit.*, pp. 36-37.
74. *Tarikh-i-Kashmir, Intikab*, Epitome of Persian translation of *Rajatarangini* of Jonaraja and Srinagar in Micro film (Munic Manuscript), RDLKUS, ff. 67a. Although Ali Shah abdicated in favour of his son Shahi Khan (Sultan Zain-ul-Abidin in July/August 1419 A.D.) but Zain-ul-Abidin's final accession took place in 1420 A.D. when he fully succeeded in setting aside the Ali Shah's efforts to reassert his authority as Sultan in the battle of Thana.

latter ignored the Sultan's abrogation of certain taxes which some of the Sayyid Maks followers collected from non-Muslim subjects for using cremation ground.[75] He adopted a series of measures to indicate and promote the secular attitude in states dependent relationship with its subjects and this dependence was solidified by promoting various institutions of public interest. Outwardly he put up the semblance of a Muslim ruler by seeking recognition of the Abbasiad caliph of Egypt for providing a legal basis to his authority in the eyes of Islamic orthodoxy and called himself *Amir-ul-Muminin.*[76] He also recognised, though only in theory, the existence of *Zimmis* in his kingdom by realising *Jazia* according to Islamic tradition but in actual practice he never collected even one *masha* to which it was reduced from two *pals.*[77] Sultan Zain-ul-Abidin did establish the post of *Sheikh-ul-Islam* in his domain for enforcement of *Shariat* but he never permitted his decisions regarding the state and societal matters to be influenced by the office of *Sheikh-ul-Islam.*[78] It appears that Sultan Zain-ul-Abidin was politically a liberal and he realised that the most obvious break on the affairs of state were Sayyids. He thought that an elaborate administrative system and a strong standing army was essentially needed to strengthen the basis of his power and this was impossible without the participation of non-Sayyid nobility which was the part of secular inheritance. He felt

75. Zutshi; *Op. Cit.*, p. 71.
76. *Ibid.*, p. 97, also *Journal Royal Asiatic Society of Bengal*, Vol. XLVIII, 1879, p. 284.
77. *Tarikh-i-Kashmir*, Munic Manuscripts, f. 70, Zutshi, *Op. Cit.*, p. 71.
78. Though Sayyid-ullah Shirazi was the *Qazi* (chief justice) but it was Shirya Bhatta who headed the department. Even Ganapati Gaurak appointed was *pradvivak* to further restrict Shirazis influence. Jonaraja; *Op. Cit.*, St. 853-955. Zutshi says, "We are however, placed in comparatively much better position with kings court. It was the highest court in land and presided over by Sultan trying civil and criminal cases. It was both the court of appeal and court of first instance. As the highest court its jurisdiction extended to the whole of Kashmir. It was composed of men belonging to different religions required to interpret the personal law of each individual according to his religion", Zutshi; *Op. Cit.*, pp. 121-122.

more and more concerned in rebuilding their identity. To name a few, Tilka Acharya was one of the most important official of Sultan.[79] Jaya Bhatta was the Sultans treasurer, Shriya Bhatta and Gánapati Gaurak manned the judicial administration under Sultan. Malik Autar Chand was the commander of army. Kanch-Dammara was the important city prefect.[80] The other important local nobles at his court were, Nothsoma; Yodha Bhatta, Avtar Batta, Darya Khan, Seikh-noor-ud-din, Mulla Qazi Khan, Mulla Kabir Kashmiri, Sita Kantha, Siva Bhatta, Mansur Bin Mohammad, Pandit Srivara, Mulla Ahmad Kashmiri, Mulla Nadri, Jonaraja, Karpura Bhatta, Rupya Bhatta, Sinha, Rajanak, Rig, Abmanyu, Jamil Hafiz and others.[81]

In a very little time he rationalised and reformed the administrative system and put new vigour into fiscal system. To ensures adequate economic surplus for the maintenance of states expenditure he took immense interest in agricultural production and expansion of cultivable waste. Srivara, the contemporary chronicler of Sultan quotes him "For the love that I have for my subjects I have augmented the production of my country threefold with the help of canals, extensive cultivation by other means".[82] The promotion of crafts like metal work, wood work, wood carving, paper machine, carpet weaving, book binding, stone polishing, bottle making, gold beating, window cutting, and various other activities brought new foreign forms and revolutionalised the native taste.[83]

This further gave peculiar turn to Kashmiri styles which owed much to Central Asian influence. For importing new designs and skills Sultan invited artists from Sijistan, Iraq, Samarkand, Herat, Khurasan, Gilan, Balakh, Bokhara, Gujrat

79. *Ibid.*, p. 122.
80. Nizam-ud-din Ahmad; *Tabqat*, Vol. III, pp. 652-53. *Baharistan-i-Shahi*; p. 54. Srivara; *Op. Cit.*
81. For details see Zutshi; *Op. Cit.*, pp. 67-149.
82. Srivara; Vol. VII, St. 974.
83. Zutshi; *Op. Cit.*, pp. 115-151.

and various other parts of the world.[84] Here it is necessary to mention that the relations with these countries were not only limited to exchange of periodic gifts but marked a wide spread foreign influence in peoples life and opened new phase of development in technology and economy in Kashmir. His reign saw the emergence of the new towns which grew into the regional metropolis with great concentration of officials, merchants, craftsmen and high level of commercial activity. In course of time there emerged new economic elite who aspired for political power.

In this attitude towards neighbouring regions Sultan Zain-ul-Abidin did not concentrate on mighty military activities against them for he felt that the political existence of small regions was necessary so long as they did not grow in wealth and power to challenge his legitimacy. He had no desire to dissolve them into his domain. His relations with Jasrat Khokhar, and the other feudatories of Jammu, Naushera, Rajouri, Lohara, Ladakh, Kishtwar clearly indicate that this attitude of Sultan towards them had an important ideological or legitimational justification for the existence of a political pluralism under one Sultan.[85]

Besides all these measures what distinguished Sultan Zain-ul-Abidins ideology from other Shahmir Sultans was the apparent fact that he concentrated on various aspects of education, culture, craft produce as a primary mechanism to maintain order in society. "Zain-ul-Abidin was in theory the head of an absolute monarchy concentrating all executive, legislative and judicial powers in his hands. But in practice was a kind and benevolent ruler and his rule an enlightened

---

84. *Ibid.*, pp. 55-58. The caligraphists from Samarkand and Balakh were granted assignments of land in *Pargana* Phag for their maintenance while they were in Kashmir to develop new styles of Caligraphy and painting. In painting the new patterns developed under Sultan were the circular designs, plant forms, human forms, images of goddesses and various of types of flowers and figures of birds and animals. Nizam-ud-din; *Op. Cit.*, pp. 653-659. Abul Fazl; *Ain*, Vol. II, p. 38. See also R.C. Kak; *Archaeological Survey Report*, (1906-7), pp. 163-64.
85. Haider Malik; *Op. Cit.*, p. 47. Firishta; *Op. Cit.*, p. 468. *Baharistan-i-Shahi*, pp. 29-64. Zutshi; *Op. Cit.*, pp. 79-83.

autocracy".[86]

Although the stability of Shahmir State was achieved by Sultan Zain-ul-Abidin by balancing the power of Sayyids and non-Sayyid nobility, but all this was only a brief interval. Because after his death in 1470 A.D. the medieval state lost its hegemonic position because of the cease less efforts of Sayyids and the rival factions of local nobility with new cumulative strains which pushed the medieval state in Kashmir into a vortex of complete economic and social collapse from which it was ultimately rescued by extension of Mughal rule only.

86. Zutshi; *Op. Cit.*, p. 94.

2

THE PORTUGUESE TRADE AND STATE IN SIXTEENTH CENTURY INDIA

K.S. Mathew

IN the *"Varna"* based Indian society, the merchants theoretically did not occupy a respectable position. They, in fact played an important role in converting the disposable goods into cash and other essential commodities of high value imported from other parts of the world. Therefore, the ruling class in medieval India which derived revenue chiefly from agricultural products from the land directly held by the state or assigned to the nobles by the ruler depended to a large extent on the exchange of commodities for their financial dealings. The assignees had to convert the agricultural products into cash. It were the merchants who came to their help in circumstance of this nature. Similarly the rulers who got the revenue in kind from the agriculturists and the products of the land directly owned by the state needed the help of those who dealt in commodities. Moreover the subcontinent of India having the longest coastline had both Intra Asian and Euro-Asian trade relations. The ruling class in medieval India took necessary steps to collect revenue from the exchange of goods that took place in various port-towns on the peninsular India. It was realised by them that both internal as well as external trade brought sizeable income to the treasury. Hence it is quite natural to surmise that the ruling class kept good relations with the merchants in general. In a pre-industrial society the most important source of income consisted in the exchange of goods. This became more important in the sixteenth century when the surplus products of the agricultural as well as non-agricultural sectors were taken in large volume directly to Europe and other parts of the world with the opening of the direct sea-route connecting India with the Atlantic ports and establishment of Portuguese trade on a firm footing with the peninsular India. As it is evident to everyone, in tune with the greater demand for commodities the agricultural production also was intensified. Therefore, an attempt is made here to highlight the attitude of the medieval Indian state or the state as represented by the various regional ruling classes towards trade. Chiefly contemporary sources in European languages as well as indigenous reports are made use of for the preparation of the study.

The subcontinent of India was parcelled out into various regional states during the medieval period and so it is not possible to speak of a medieval Indian state in abstract. Consequently any one interested in highlighting the attitudes of Indian state towards trade especially international trade during this period has to deal with that of various regional rulers towards the trade.

Chronologically, the Zamorin of Calicut on the Malabar coast was the first Indian ruler to come in contact with the Portuguese who came to India primarily to establish commercial relations. The fleet of Vasco de Gama consisting of four vessels reached Calicut on May 20, 1498 with a letter addressed by Dom Manuel to the Zamorian. The latter who used to give whatever assistance possible to the merchants coming from various parts of the world like Mecca, Tenasserim, Pegu, Ceylon, Turkey, Egypt, Persia, Ethiopia as well as several parts of the subcontinent of India extended a warm welcome to the Portuguese, Moreover, the Zamorin sent a letter on cadjan leaves to the King of Portugal requesting him to send certain commodities regularly from Portugal to Calicut. He did not probably envisage that this would be the beginning of a revolutionary change in the usual pattern of trade conducted in his port. Therefore, when Pedro Alvares Cabral came to Calicut with a large fleet in 1500 A.D. he did not hesitate to permit him to open a Portuguese factory at Calicut. After several rounds of discussions a commercial treaty between the Portuguese and the Zamorin was signed, one copy of which was on a silver plate stamped with golden seal and the other on copper plate stamped with brass seal. The former was taken to the King of Portugal and the latter was kept in the Portuguese factory at Calicut headed by Aires Correa.[1]

As the Portuguese fleet did not succeed in getting the required commodities while the Arab ships were laden with large volume of spices, Cabral complained to the Zamorin. The King permitted him to search the Arab ships. Subsequently, an Arab ship was captured on account of which there ensued fight between the Portuguese and the Arabs. The Portuguese factory was razed to the ground and about fifty Portuguese men along with the factor put to death.

Being informed of the unfriendly attitude of the Zamorin or rather lack of special treatment to the Portuguese on the part of the King of Calicut, the Portuguese King sent a large fleet consisting of twenty five vessels under Vasco de Gama in 1502 A.D. to take the Zamorin to task and to avenge the merchants for their attitude. The indigence of Vasco de Gama did not know any bounds and, therefore, before starring any negotiations with the Zamorin the evacuation of all Arab merchants as well as that of the Muslim merchants was insisted upon by Vasco de Gama. The King interested in deriving as much profit as possible from the trade in his port could not accede to the request made by the Portuguese that his port should be exclusively reserved for the Portuguese and all other merchants should be driven away. In unequivocal terms he stated that his port would be open to anyone interested in trade and commerce.[2]

---

1. Montalbodo, *Paesi Nouvamente retrovati & Novo Mondo da Alberico Vesputio Florentino intitulato* (Reprinted with Fascimile), Princeton, 1916, pp. 86, 90; *Cronica do Descobrimento e Conquista da India pelos Portuguese*, Coimbra, 1974, p. 21.
2. Thome Lopes; *"Navegacao as Indias Orientais"* in *Colleccoa de Noticias Dara a Historia e Geografia das Nacoes Ultramarinas que Vivem nos dominios Portugueses on ihes sao visinhas*, Tom, II, No. 1 & 2, Lisboa, 1812, p. 1871, Joao de Barros, *Da Asia, Decada*, I. Part II, Lisboa, 1973, p. 49.

Here one can understand the attitude of a medieval state towards the Portuguese traders who wanted to have a special treatment on the bias of a treaty signed between two powers. The Zamorin can be taken as a genuine representative of the medieval Indian state which did not bother about anything except the advantages one could derive from trade. He was not concerned with any particular group of merchants. He extended facilities for trade to anyone irrespective of any nationality or community. Portuguese King entered on a treaty with an Indian ruler, in effect recognising the equality of status. In fact, the Portuguese writers who propounded theories supporting the exclusive claim of the Portuguese to have trade and commerce, did not recognise the equality of status for the Indian rulers since they were considered by them unlawful occupants of the Kingdom as well as the Indian Ocean regions being outside the Christian faith.

Vasco de Gama being frustrated in his attempts to convince the Zamorin of the necessity of providing special treatment to the Portuguese traders, took certain steps which were totally alien to the commercial world. He massacred a number of people and cut their heads, arms and legs and put them in a ship and sent to the Zamorin "as a present" along with a letter in the local language stating that he came to purchase good commodities from Calicut, but what he got was being sent as "Gift".[3] The Zamorin being mindful of the damage done by the Portuguese to his port took septs to retaliate the King of Cochin who extended a warm welcome to the Portuguese. Seven naval battles were waged against the King of Cochin and the Portuguese, though the Zamorin could not meet with a definite victory.[4]

Since the Zamorin began to suffer a lot of loss on account of the disturbance caused to the commercial prosperity of his kingdom as well as to the port of Calicut, he went so far as to send his envoy Maymame to *Q'ansawh alo Ghawri*, the

3. Thome Lopes, *Op. Cit.*, p. 109; Barros, *Op. Cit., Decada I*, Part, II, p. 53.
4. Barros; *Op. Cit., Decade I*, Part II, pp. 77ff.

Sultan of Cairo, to join hands to oust the Portuguese traders from the Indian Ocean regions.[5] He sent forty warships to fight against the Portuguese at Chaul in 1508 A.D. and to make the trade free from the political intervention of the Portuguese. With the help of the fleet of the Turks, the Gujaratis, Bijapur and Ahmednagar, the Portuguese were defeated at Chaul.[6]

The fight between the Zamorin and the Portuguese traders came to an end temporarily with the death of the then Zamorin in 1513 A.D. and the installation of a friendly ruler in the throne of Calicut by the Portuguese. Afonso de Albuquerque through his nephew Garcia de Noronha managed to conclude a commercial treaty with the new Zamorin and obtained permission to open a factory and a fortress at Calicut. The local ruler sent his Ambassador to the king of Portugal insisting that the treaty should be signed by the king himself, which was done on February 26, 1515 A.D. The treaty stipulated that certain commodities should be sent to Calicut from Portugal, and spice and other commodities from Calicut should be despatched to Portugal. However, it was agreed that the Portuguese would pay the customs duties to the King of Calicut for the commodities they purchased while the buyers of the commodities from the Portuguese were expected to pay the duries to the king of Portugal. All the Muslim ships coming from any part of the world as well as the Portuguese ships bringing horses or elephants to the port of Calicut were supposed to pay the usual duties to the Zamorin. The Zamorin agreed to see that certain quantity of pepper and other spices required by the Portuguese were delivered at the price fixed with the merchants at Cochin and Cannanore in 1503 A.D. The duties

---

5. Fernao Lopes de Castanheda; *Historia de Descobrimento e Conquista da India Pelos Portugueses*, Livro I, Coimbra, 1924, p. 384.
6. For a detailed study of the confrontation, refer; K.S. Mathew; *"The First Mercantile Battle in the Indian Ocean: The Afro-Asian Front Against the Portuguese (1508-1509)", II Seminario Internacional de Historia Indo-Portuguese–Actas*, Lasboa, 1985, pp. 179-85.

were to be paid in cash to the Zamorin though provision was made for the purchase by exchange of goods. The price of ginger was not fixed and so the Portuguese were expected to purchase it according to the price agreed with the cultivators or merchants from time to time.

The Zamorin of Calicut insisted on equality of status and therefore, he wanted the King of Portugal himself to sign the treaty. He sent his own Ambassador to Portugal and requested the Ambassador from there to be sent to his court. As medieval state depended to a large extent on the revenue from agricultural sector as well as from the exchange of the agricultural products, the Zamorin formulated the terms and conditions of the customs duties on the exchange of his commodities. The Zamorin further insisted on the exchange of his commodities. The Zamorin further insisted that he should get the entire income from the customs house as well as that from the issue of *Cartazes*. So he made a representation in 1520 through Coje Byquyin asking the Portuguese to consider the matter of income from *cartazes* and from the custom houses in the same way as in Cochin and Cannanore.[7] Just as any medieval ruler of India, the Zamorin wanted to get the income from the trade conducted at his port.

The next medieval ruler of the subcontinent of India who welcomed the Portuguese traders was the King of Cochin, who was considered a vassal of the Zamorin and was looking for a chance for breaking the shackles of feudal ties with the ruler of Calicut. He envisaged the possibility of accumulating large capital through encouraging trade and commerce at his port. Therefore, he welcomed the Portuguese traders with open arms and went so far as to stand as a mediator between the Portuguese and the local traders. When Pedro Alvares Cabral reached Cochin in December 1500 A.D., after having a tough time with the Zamorin, the king provided necessary facilities to load all the

7. *Cartas; Op. Cit.*, Tom; I, pp. 133, 188, 409; Tom; II, p. 113; Tom, IV, pp. 31-33; Bicker; *Op. Cit.*, pp. 22-23.

ships with necessary cargo.[8] The treaty of peace and friendship with the Portuguese king was signed with the provision to open a factory at Cochin.[9]

The interest in deriving profit from trade shown by the King of Cochin was clearly envinced in 1501 A.D. when Joao de Nova found himself helpless in getting the required cargo from Cochin. The Portuguese traders did not have the cash to buy pepper and spices. The King of Cochin stood as a surety and got pepper, ginger, cinnamon and cloth from the local merchants for them to be taken to Portugal.[10]

In spite of threats on the part of the Zamorin, the King of Cochin went on extending all the facilities to the Portuguese traders as he was fully convinced that trade of this nature would bring great profit to his exchequer. He permitted the Portuguese even to establish a well fortified fortress in Cochin. Against the existing traditions he allowed the Portuguese to build it with stone and mortar. During the naval confrontations with the Zamorin, the King of Cochin lost two of his uncles for the sake of the Portuguese. It was the motive of getting profit through the Portuguese trade with Cochin that he submitted himself as a vassal to the King of Portugal in 1505 A.D. at the hands of the Portuguese Viceroy. Even though he was a staunch Hindu he did not mind in taking an oath of fealty to the King of Portugal touching the Holy Bible of the Christians. The ceremonies of coronation by the Portuguese officials continued to be in vogue even in the seventeenth century. Being afraid of losing the income from trade he kept the Portuguese away from entering into a *rapprochement* with the Zamorin of Calicut. His indignation knew no bounds when he heard that treaty between the King

8. *Letter of Giovanni Francesco de Affaitadi in Marino Sanuto, I, Diarii de Marino Sanuto: 1496-1533,* edited by G. Berchet R. Fulin and Alii, Venice, 1897-1903, Tom, IV; *Op. Cit.,* Col. 68, see also *letter of Thomas, Jaballah, Jacobus and Denha* written in Syriac language and preserved in Bibliotheca Apostolica Vaticana, Col. Syr. 5, Tom 2, biblioth Orient, p. 488 and reproduced in Syriac with a Latin translation by Joseph Simon Assemanus in *Bibliotheca Orientalis,* Tom, III, Part I, Roma, 1725, p. 596.
9. *Cronica do Descobrimento e Conquista de India pelos Portuguese,* p. 25.
10. Sanuto, *I Diarii,* Tom, IV, Col. 664.

of Portugal and the Zamorin was concluded. He wrote letter after letter to the King of Portugal against the *entente* between the Zamorin and the Portuguese.[11] Despite the protest, the Portuguese King ratified the treaty. So the King of Cochin wrote in 1516 A.D. that it would be impossible for him to arrange spices at the price fixed by the Portuguese, which was quite below the market rate. He alluded to the fact that the spice were taken to places other than the Portuguese factories by the local merchants on account of the low price offered by the Portuguese.[12] Being aware of the advantages that could accrue from the Portuguese trade at his port, the King of Cochin did not want to break off the relations permanently with the Portuguese and continued to be friendly with them.

The amicable contact with the Portuguese cherished for over a century and a half by the king of Cochin speaks for the attitude of the rulers of medieval India towards the Portuguese traders. He knew that in the context of the sixteenth century it was only the Portuguese and the local merchants who would help him in converting the disposable output of the agrarian sector and bring the required cash to him. Though on the whole merchants were not held in high esteem by the people of higher caste, the King of Cochin used to be extraordinarily friendly with the merchants like Mamale Marakkar and Cherina Marakkar, in whose company he used to visit the Portuguese Viceroy at his quarters.[13] He advanced loan and sometimes supplied commodities on credit to the Portuguese since he was fully aware of the possibilities of getting profit from the trade. In fact, it was his continuous collaboration with the Portuguese traders and the subsequent enrichment of the kingdom that made him an independent king totally cut away from his feudalistic relations with the Zamorin.

The King of Cannanore whose kingdom had a large supply of ginger, pepper and a number of other oriental

11. *Cartas de Afonso de Albuquerque,* Tom, III, pp. 39, 73-84; Tom IV, pp. 71-73.
12. *Ibid.,* Tom, IV, pp. 71-73.
13. *Ibid.,* Tom, III, p. 257.

spices, welcomed the Portuguese to his port and offered them a site to establish a factory and later in 1505 A.D. a fortress. A treaty between the King of Cannanore and Portugal was concluded.[14] Apart from occasional confrontations, the king kept friendly relations with the Portuguese and often purchased *Cartazes,* from them to sent his ships to the Red Sea and Persian Gulf areas to import certain number of horses. It is worth noting that he agreed to purchase *Cartazes* (passes) from the Portuguese for conducting seaborne trade and rendering his ships free from being captured by the Portuguese.

While Pedro Alvares Cabral was busy loading the ships at Cochin in 1501 A.D., the ruler of Quilon, south of Calicut sent messengers requesting him to send ships to Quilon for the export of pepper. Though Cabral had to excuse himself on account of the time and availability of required cargo in Cochin, Afonso de Albuqerque in 1503 A.D. accepted the invitation and got a large volume of pepper from Quilon. As the Portuguese did not offer market rates for pepper but on the contrary insisted on the price fixed in early 1503 A.D. with Cannanore and Cochin, ruler of Quilon connived at the flow of pepper from Quilon via Aryankavu Pass[15] to Tamil Nadu and Goa the Coromandel coast. When pressure was brought to the king by Portuguese, he permitted them to establish a fortress and make compensation for the damage caused to the Portuguese. He agreed to see to it that the stipulated quantity of pepper and other spices were delivered to the Portuguese factory at Quilon. Treatment of this nature on the part of the ruler of Quilon was chiefly due to the conviction that active trade of the Portuguese with Quilon would bring large amount of profit and subsequent prosperity to his kingdom.

Some of the medieval rulers of India who had their nobility actively involved in overseas trade initially were reluctant to welcome the Portuguese to their ports since they

---

14. *Ibid.*, Tom, II, p. 400.
15. *Kerala Palama* (Malayalam), Kottayam, 1868, pp. 140ff.

insisted on preferential treatments. The rulers of Bijapur, Ahmednagar and Gujarat who were from commercialised regions of India organised a united front as mentioned earlier against the Portuguese in 1508 A.D. When they realised that the Portuguese would conduct trade with the force of arms, important nobles like Malik Ayyaz of Diu. Offered sites for the Portuguese factory. It was the naval superiority emanating especially from the better quality of artillery used by the Portuguese that made the rulers of Gujarat and Ahmadnagar permit the Portuguese to establish commercial relations with the regions under their authority. A Portuguese factory was established in Diu in the second decade of the sixteenth century and a fortress in Chaul. At last Bahadur Shah, the Sultan of Gujarat offered a site for a Portuguese fortress at Bassein and later in Diu. But Malik Gopi, another powerful noble of *sultanate* of Gujarat welcomed the Portuguese on account of his animosity towards Malik Ayyaz of Diu who reaped unimaginable profit from the trade conducted at Diu. Moreover, he was involved in long distance trade in large quantity with Southeast Asian countries especially Malacca. He offered to be a mediator between the Portuguese and the Sultan of Gujarat for cordial relations, but the court intrigues made acute by Malik Ayyaz brought about the fall of Malik Gopi. At last through force of arms in the fourth decade of the sixteenth century, the Portuguese managed to establish factories and fortresses on the coastal regions of Gujarat and conducted flourishing trade.

Adil Shah, the ruler of Bijapur initially put up stiff fight against the Portuguese. But when he was busily engaged in confrontations with the Emperor of Vijayanagar, the Portuguese took over Goa which was one of the important centres of trade in horses from Jida, Aden and other places in West Asia. After a few months, Adil Shah ogranised a battle to oust the Portuguese from Goa. Despite repeated efforts he failed to achieve the target. The Portuguese saw to it that horses were not supplied to him from Goa. As there was no possibility of getting rid of the Portuguese, he signed a treaty of peace and friendship with them. In view of the long standing friendship very diplomatically cherished, Adil Shah collected *Cartazes* for his ships to be sent to Mecca, Ormuz, and other places. Most of the ships belonging to him used to leave from the port of Dabul. However, he was not allowed to carry Trade in cinnamon and copper from Ceylon.[16]

The Nizam Shah of Ahmadnagar in collaboration with the ruler of Bijapur and Malik Ayyaz of Diu fought against the Portuguese in the first decade of the sixteenth century because they found that their interest in trade would be jeopardised if the Portuguese were given facilities for conducting monopolistic trade. This prompted him to take part in the naval confrontation in 1508 A.D. in which the Portuguese forces were routed mercilessly. Subsequently after meeting with failure in 1509 A.D. he began to give tributes to the Portuguese and to be friendly with them. He permitted them to open a factory and later a fortress in Chaul which was a great centre of trade in horses as well as textiles. Even when the Sultan of Gujarat at the insistence of Malik Ayyaz fought against the Portuguese on account of the fortress being established by them at Chaul, Nizam Shah remained loyal to the Portuguese traders. In view of the treaties between the Portuguese and Nizam Shah, the latter was given regularly seven *cartazes* (Passes) for his ships to be sent to Malacca, Ormuz and Mecca. His ships were allowed to carry a few pieces of arms and ammunitions for defence. But certain items like copper, lead, iron, pepper, cinnamon from Ceylon, saltpeter, Turks and Abyssinians were not allowed to be taken in the vessels for which Nizam Shah got the passes from the Portuguese.[17]

The ruler of Vijayanagar kept friendly relations with the Portuguese even after Goa passed into the hands of the Portuguese in 1510 A.D. With a view of getting more horses to his land, Krishna Deva Raya permitted the Portuguese to establish a factory at Bhatkal in his territory in 1510 A.D. Ramraja of Vijayanagar concluded a treaty with the

16. Julio Firmino Judice Biker; *Op. Cit.*, Tom, IV, pp. 181-82; MSS. HAG Codex No. 1043, fols. 67-71 for the *cartazes* issued in 1621.
17. MSS. Goa Historical Archieves, Codex, No. 1043, folio 59-62.

Portuguese whereby the supply of horses to Bijapur was stopped. Large number of horses were bought by the ruler of Vijayanagar costing 400 to 600 *crusados* each. It was calculated that the emperor of Vijayanagar had more than 20,000 horses.[18]

There were several diamond mines in the vicinity of the city of Vijayanagar. Therefore, the Portuguese merchants visited Vijayanagar and were treated very friendly by the emperor because of the advantages he could derive from the trade with the Portuguese.

18. Joao de Barros; *Op. Cit.*, Decada II, Part I, Lisboa, 1777, p. 210; Lodovico di Varthema, *The Itinerary of Ludovico di Varthema of Boloqna from 1500-1508*, London, 1928, p. 51.

3

THE MUGHAL STATE IN 17TH CENTURY PUNJAB

Chetan Singh

IF a scholar were to search for water marks in the development of historical writing on medieval India, the contribution of the 'Aligarh school' could very justifiably lay claim to such a distinction. While the work of the Aligarh Scholars covers a wide spectrum of historical processes of the Mughal period, it is bound quite closely by their basic understanding of the Mughal state; an understanding that has acquired the status of an almost undisputed assumption among a large number of historians today. The Mughal state, in brief, is perceived as a systematically centralized one, both theoretically and in reality. It is seen as one that had acquired the power to enforce uniformity of government in all parts of the empire and was sustained by its ability to appropriate a large portion of the economic surplus generated within its frontiers. The administrative machinery (both offical and quasi official) involved in the maintenance of this 'Mughal system' presents a picture of truly gigantic proportions, yet one that is portrayed as almost uniformly conforming to elaborately formulated methods of functioning. The works of Irfan Habib, S. Nurul Husan, M. Athar Ali and N.A. Siddiqi apart from the host of others, are among the more impressive contributions in this context.[1]

1. *The Agrarian System of Mughal India* (Bombay, 1963); *An Atlas of the Mughal*

(Contd. to next page)

A substantial part of the understanding of the Aligarh historians seems to have been, in a way, consolidated in the *Cambridge Economic History of India*[2] which reiterated many of the fundamentals of medieval Indian history as represented in thier earlier works. Here we may also refer in passing to J.F. Rechards' investigation regarding the nature of the Mughal state as it expanded to certain parts of the Deccan.[3] Richards, however, is concerned with a region that was not truely representative of the classical Mughal imperial system.

Juxtapositioned with the pioneering endeavours which unveiled the remarkable intricacies of state and society in India during the seventeenth century, the eighteenth century began to appear as one of decline or at best of century shrouded in mystery. Much by way of correcting this misconception has been done by C.A. Bayly's work on late eighteenth century and nineteenth century north India.[4] Primarily concerned with social and economic change occurring in parts of upper India between 1770 and 1870, Bayly dwells upon some trends that dominate his period of study, but which appear to trace their first stirring to an earlier time. The more significant of these, from our point of view, were the process by which the 'intermediate groups' were 'consolidating' themselves between the state and peasantry[5], and the emergence of a situation in which the 'great Muslim military and administrative families who had served the Mughals at the centre' were gaining much from the 'fluid politics of the period'.[6] Undoubtedly, Mughal imperialism

---

(Contd. from previous page)

Empire (Delhi, 1982); S. Nurul Hassan; *Some Thoughts on Agrarian Relations in Mughal India* (Delhi, 1973); M. Athar Ali; *The Mughal Nobility under Aurangzeb* (Bombay, 1966); *The Apparatus of Empire* (Delhi, 1985); N.A. Siddiqi; *Land Revenue Administration under the Mughal*, 1700-1790 (Bombay, 1970).

2. *Cambridge Economic History of India*, Vol. 1, Tapan Raychaudhuri and Irfan Habib (Eds.) (Cambridge, 1982).
3. J.F. Richards, *Mughal Administration in Golconda* (Oxford, 1975).
4. C.A. Bayly; *Rulers, Townsmen and Bazars, North Indian Society in the Age of British Expansion, 1770-1870* (Cambridge, 1983).
5. *Ibid.*, pp. 7-8.
6. *Ibid.*, p. 12.

offered to the more adventurous spirits, power, wealth and honour on a scale almost unprecedented in Indian history. If Mughal decline is to be traced to the empire's inability to support its servants in splendour, it is equally likely that the long period of imperial glory should influence in a most fundamental manner those who had most benefited from it. It is possible that the 'rooted service gentry;' and the a crumbling imperial edifice existed, even if in an embryonic form, during the seventeenth century.

Among the scholars who have more directly questioned centralized character of the medieval Indian state are Burton Stein and Frank Perlin.[7] Their questioning, too, has been directed at the fundamental levels of the social organization of production, surplus extraction and the formation of local socio-political elites. An examination at these levels would, by all means, reveal with greater clarity the true essence of the state. It is in this context that the study of the medieval Indian state appears to have taken an interesting turn. So divergent from the original conception of the nature of the medieval India state have been conclusions of Burton Stein that an entirely new dimension has been added to the existing state of historiography; albeit strongly disputed by some scholars.[8] Stein's argument, simply speaking, is that while the Mughal state has so far been taken to be unitary in character, state formation in reality was for more complex. To put it in his

7. Burton Stein; *Peasant State and Society in Medieval South India* Oxford University Press, Delhi, 1980; *"Politics, Peasants and the Deconstruction of Feudalism in Medieval India"*, in T.J. Byres and Harbans Mukhia (Eds.), *Feudalism and Non-European Societies* (London, 1985); pp. 54-86. Also *"State Formation and Economic Reconsidered, Comparison, with a Diversion on Counter Ideologies and Corporate Institutions in Late Pre-Colonial India"*, in *Feudalism and Non-European Societies,* pp. 87-167. *"State Formation Reconsidered", Modern Asian Studies,* 19.3 (1985), pp. 415-80.
8. For some of the arguments pertaining to this debate see Burton Stein, *Peasant State and Society in Medieval South India,* R. Champakalakshmi, *'Peasant State and Society in Medieval South India'* A Review Article', *Indian Economic and Social History Review,* Vol. xviii, Nos. 3 and 4, pp. 411-26. D.N. Jha; *"Relevance of 'Peasant State and Society' to Pallava-Cola Times", Indian Historical Review,* Vol. vii, Nos. 1 and 2, pp. 74-94.

words; 'The unitary state with a single authoritative centre, a single administrative corps, a centralized concentration of coercive means and a fixed territory does not comprehend all state forms; it neglects those which I and some others call 'segmentary' including political formations variously denominated as '*Feudal*' or as '*patrimonial*' sates.[9]

Also worth bearing in mind are the observations of Frank Perlin whose critique of modern historiography pertaining to the Mughal period imposes the necessity of a reconsideration of the existing established approach.[10] He refers to the 'distortions arising from a view taken from within one or another system (Caste, kinship, *jajmani, jagir* one or another administrative code or arguably "things Mughal". Perlin argues that 'these distortions systematically affect perception of other categories of social life either by denying their existence, peripheralising their importance, or by putting them aside into another pigeon hole for "further consultation" or for a different kind of specialist."[11]

From the point of view of the Mughal state, however, the work of these two scholars remains by and large peripheral. Undoubtedly, the questions and possibilities they raise are pertinent, but their area of study and the sources utilized prevent them from scrutinizing the 'Mughal system' either at the height of its power or in the region of the northern plains which formed its heartland.

More relevantly placed, both from the point of view of source material and the region of study, is Muzaffar Alam's very recently published work pertaining to the Mughal crisis in Punjab and Awadh during the first half of the eighteenth

9. Burton Stain; '*State Formation and Economy Reconsidered*', p. 388.
10. Frank Perlin; '*State Formation Reconsidered*'. Amidst this critique of the state of historiography, Perlin argues that context has been sacrificed to 'a dubious focus on inner workings, logics and principle', and that, 'a particular document tends therefore to be read as a representation of a greater system at work rather than as marks of time and place sited events which initially need to be set within local historical and structural contexts before being used for comparison and explanation', p. 420.
11. *Ibid.*, pp. 428-9.

century.[12] Deriving most of his information from Persian sources, Alam scrutinized the manner in which the Mughal state was being transformed in the very region that was considered integral to its survival as a dominant political entity in India.[13] What is more significant from our point of view, however, is his observation that 'political integration in Mughal India was, up to a coordinating agency between conflicting communities and various indigenous socio-political systems at different levels'. The nobility on its part, felt inconvenienced by the policy of regular transfer of *jagirs* and its resistance to such transfers meant that the policy was left unimplemented in a number of cases in the seventeenth century'.[14] The most pertinent possibilities concerning the nature of the Mughal state in the thrust of the nobles actions in our period, and their endeavour towards independent political alignments with the *zamindars* in order to carve out their own fortunes were not absolutely incompatible with earlier developments.[15]

If the origins of the ultimate fragmentation of the Mughal empire are to be, in a way, traced back to the seventeenth century, certain doubts begin to arise about the degree to which the mughal state was centralized. This paper dwells upon some features of the Mughal administrative system

12. Muzaffar Alam; *The Crisis of Empire in Mughal North India, Awadh and the Punjab 1707-1718*, Oxford University Press, New Delhi, 1986.
13. This work emphasizes the socio-political changes that were taking place within the Mughal imperical system and which combined with other factors to constitute the 'processes of regional restructuring'. Among these changes by way of example were the emergence of the '*Jagir-i-mahal-i-watan*' and the 'long-term *jagir* holdings'. It is pointed out that 'the *madad-i ma'ash* holders made a bid to turn their grants into *zamindaris* without forfeiting their existing privileges and perquisites. The *jagirdar*, too, aspired to a permanent holding so that he could build his own base in the region'. Quite rightly Alam points out that 'these developments violated the classical Mughal concept of imperial authority, as seen in the seventeenth century, undermined the prospects of its survival and reinforce the course of provincial autonomy'. *Ibid.*, pp. 13-15. Chapters I and II deal at length with these questions.
14. *Ibid.*, p. 5.
15. *Ibid.*, p. 6.

which appear outwardly to be the most obvious centralizing factors. Important in this respect would be the organization and functioning of the provincial administration; an aspect of administration which would reflect the degree and nature of centralized 'bureaucratic' control. Seventeenth-century Punjab has therefore, in this paper been made the specific subject of study.[16] Presumably this effort would be what Perlin calls a 'view from within' and hence likely to suffer from the logical shortcomings of such an approach. What balances this handicap, however, is the fact that our objective here, in the first place, is not a total reconstruction of the medieval (Mugal) state formation. While recognizing the imperative of such a reconstruction an attempt has here been made to consider whether even within the existing traditional historiographical framework, the Mughal state was indeed as centralized in essence as its from might suggest.[17] Optimistically speaking, it might perhaps be possible to obtain a different insight even from within the traditional framework without abandoning it in totality.

Mughal provincial government was marked not only by the existence of fairly large 'bureaucracy', but also by the establishment of very detailed methods and procedures which governed its functioning. A reasonably well demarcated hierarchy of officials along with their respective functional and territorial jurisdiction had, in fact come into existence quite early during Mughal rule in India. Details regarding the large number of imperial official at the provincial level, as also

16. The areas taken up for examination are those which constituted the British province of Punjab. These, therefore, included the entire Mughal *suba* of Lahore, and parts of *suba* Multan and *suba* Delhi.

17. In his massive work on the administrative machinery of the Mughals, M. Athar Ali; *The Apparatus of Empire, Award of Ranks, Offices and Titles to the Mughal Nobility (1574-1658)*, Oxford University Press, Delhi, 1985, once again reasserts the centralized nature of the Mughal state. According to him *mansab* system represented one facet of the extreme degree of systematization and centralization reached in the Mughal empire. It was similarly reflected in the uniformity enforced in the post and functions there to in all parts of the empire', p. xxi.

the rules and procedures pertaining to their appointment, functions and jurisdictions can be found in some of the authoritative works on administration.[18] We need not here delve into these details. While recognizing the vast and complicated nature of the Mughal 'bureaucracy', this paper seeks to utilize for the present purpose two aspects of Mughal provincial administration which are most commonly encountered by a researcher scrutinizing contemporary Persian chronicles. The first aspect if the frequent reference to the transfer of Mughal officials to different posts and places, and the second is the repeated mention of the office of *faujdar* who appears to have been the most effective local official and upon whom apparently rested the onus of maintaining imperial authority at the lower levels.

We may first consider the Mughal policy of periodically transferring imperial official; a policy which has come to be recognised by historians as one that was most regularly practised by the Mughal Emperors. The principal that lay behind the establishment of this policy was to prevent officials from developing strong local roots in a manner that was likely to pose a threat to the empire's stability and integrity. Abul Fazl, in fact elaborates this principle by means of an interesting analogy.

It is not hidden from the hearts of the far-seeing and the clearsighted that the spiritual garland-twiners of sovereignty (i.c. kings) resemble gardeners. As gardeners adorn garderns with trees and move them from one place to another, and reject many and irrigate others, and labour to rear them to a proper size, and extirpate bad trees and lop off evil branches and remove trees that are too large, and graft some upon others, and gather their various fruits and flowers and enjoy

18. The matter has been quite thoroughly dealt with in P. Saran, *The Provincial Government of the Mughals 1526-1658*, Allahabad, 1941; M. Athar Ali; *The Mughal Nobility under Aurangzeb*, Bombay, 1966; some other works of relevance are Abdul Aziz; *The Mansabdari System and the Mughal Army*, Lahore, 1945; Jadunath Sarkar, *Mughal Administration*, Calcutta, 1952.

their shade when necessary, and do thing which are established in the science of horticulture. . .[19]

The actual context in which this was written was the removal of the Akta Khail from *suba* Lahore by Akbar. Even keeping in mind Abul Fazl's tendencey of providing an ideological justification for the political actions of Akbar,[20] it does seem very likely that the policy of transfers was in principle directed towards preventing any particular section of the Mughal nobility from becoming too powerful in a region.

The regularity with which contemporary Persian chronicles refer to the transfer of imperial official and the significance that was, probably, attached to such transfers from the viewpoint of statecraft, might lead one to imagine that on account of frequent transfers the Mughals bureaucracy was unable to develop regional moorings. This, however, might not have been entirely true. Transfers of official did indeed take place, but this did not always or even commonly involve shifting an official from one end of the empire to the other. By examining instances to transfers in Punjab during the seventeenth century it might be possible to discover their exact nature and geographical extent. It would be worth considering whether the policy of shifting officials from one place to another, so as to keep them from becoming too powerful, was effectively practiced. Most of the available information pertains to the region of Shahjahan, perhaps due to the nature of our sources. The conclusions drawn, however, need not necessarily have relevance limited to that particular reign. Indeed, there is a possibility that the conclusions would be reflection of trends stretching over a longer time span.

At the top of the provincial 'bureaucratic' hierarchy was the *subadar* who was best placed to concentrate power in his hands if he was so inclined. In accordance with the policy

19. Abdul Fazl, *Akbarnama* (H. Beveridge (tr) Reprint, New Delhi, 1979), Vols. 3. See Vol. II, pp. 486-7. Hereafter referred to as Akbarnama.
20. Harbans Mukhia; *Historians and Historiography During the Reign of Akbar* (Vikas Publishing House, New Delhi, 1976), pp. 72-84.

earlier elaborated by Abul Fazl, the *Subadars* of both Lahore and Multan were regularly transferred.[21] Only occasionally are nobles known to have remained in one place as *Subadars* for a relatively long period. For example, in *Suba* Lahore the longest term as *Subadar* was probably served by Wazir Khan during the reign of Shahajahan.[22] In *Suba* Multan Qulij Khan Turani seems to have functioned as the *Subadar* for the longest period of seven years.[23] Every transfer, however, did not mean that and absolute newcomer to the area came to succeed the previous incumbent. To the contrary the names of some of these officials that they, in fact belonged to areas lying within Punjab. Examples of such a nature were Ghazi Beg Tarkhan, Dilawar Khan Kakar and Khwaja Main.[24] It is quite likely that their familiarity with and greater influence in the region played an important role in their appointment; the Mughal policy of preventing *Subadars* from developing local roots seems to have been conveniently ignored here. That locally influential people were actually appointed to the *Subadari* of the region seems to militate against the principles that lay behind the policy of transferring officials.

---

21. The details on this regard can be found in M. Athar Ali; *The Apparatus of Empire*, pp. xxxii-xi (Tables, 4, 5 and 6).
22. Though there is no direct reference to the exact length of his tenure as *subadar*, the available information seems to point in this direction. Muhammad Salih Kamboh, *Amal-i-Salih* or *Shahjahan Namah of Muhammad Salik Kamboh*, Gulam Yazdani (Ed.) (Bibliotheca Indica, Calcutta, 1912-46), Vols. 3. Hereafter referred to as Amal-i-Salih. See Vol. II, pp. 11, 309. See also Shah Nawaz Khan, *The Ma'athir-ul-Umara*, being Biographies of the Muhammadan and Hindu officers of the Timurid Sovereigns of India from 1500 to about 1780 A.D. H. Beveridge (tr) Revised, annotated and completed by Baini Prasad, Vol. I, Royal Asiatic Society of Bengal, Calcutta, 1911-41, Vol. II, Asiatic Society, Calcutta, 1952. Hereafter referred to as *Ma'athir-ul-Umara*. See Vol. II, p. 982.
23. *Amal-i-Shalih*, Vol. II, p. 4, 10.
24. Ghazi Beg Tarkha was *Subadar* of Multan during the early years of Jahangir's reign. Nuruddin Muhammad Jahangir, *Tuzuk-i-Jahangiri*. See Vol. I, p. 71. Dilawar Khan Kakar held the *subadari* of Lahore around the year 1605. See Khwaja Kamgar Hussaini; *Ma'asir-i-Jahangiri*, Azra Alavi (Ed.), Bombay, 1978, p. 70. Hereafter referred to as *Ma'asir-i-Jahangiri*. See also *Ma'athir-ul-Ummara*, Vol. I, p. 488, *Tuzuk-i-Jahangiri*, Vol. I, pp. 49, 77. Khwaja Main was *Subadar* of Lahore in 1655-56, see *Amali-i-Salih*, Vol. III, p. 232.

It furthermore appears that there came into existence a circle of officials who, though they were shifted from one place to another, were never really removed from the region as such. The repeated mention in our sources of some officials being reappointed to different positions within Punjab suggests that despite frequent transfers their association with a particular region continued. Punjab being a fairly large geographical area, it is possible that the regional experience of many of those officials was often utilised by placing them in one official position after another within the region itself. There were also instances of Mughal nobles being reappointed to the same position after a time gap. It is quite likely that during their absence from Punjab these nobles were to be found at the imperial court rather than occupying an office in some other province of the empire.

Among the instances of nobles being reappointed to the same position in a particular *Suba* after a time gap we know of Najabat Khan Mirza Shuja who was appointed *Subadar* of Multan in 1638-39 even though he had been *naib-subadar* of the *Suba* in 1630-31.[25] There were also others like Qulij Khan Turani, Said Khan Bahadur and Lashkar Khan who served as *Subadars* of Multan for at least two terms each.[26]

In *Suba* Lahore, however, we find fewer *Subadars* serving a second term. In addition to Said Khan Bahadur who served as *Subadar* of Lahore for two terms we have two instances of Princes Muhammad Mu'azzam and Muhammad Azam being appointed as *Subadar* of Lahore for more than one term each.[27]

---

25. *Amal-i-Salih*, Vol. II, p. 308, *Ma'athir-ul-Umara*, Vol. II, pp. 365-6.
26. For Qulij Khan Turani, *Amal-i-Salih*, Vol. II, pp. 4, to 341, *Ma'athir-ul-Umara*, Vol. II, p. 543. For Said Khan Bahadur; *Amal-i-Salih*, Vol. II, pp. 362, 502, *English Factories in India*, W. Foster (Ed.), London (New Series), see Vol. 1646-50, p. 118, *Ma'athir-ul-Umara*, Vol. II, p. 678. For Lashkar Khan, Muhammad Kazim, *Alamgirnama* Mawlawis Khadim Hussain and Abd-al-Hai, Bibliotheca Indica, (Calcutta, 1868), see Vol. I, p. 485, (hereafter referred to as *Alimgirnama*); Saqi Musta'id, Khan, *Ma'asir-i-Alamgiri*, Jadunath Sarkar (Tr) (Calcutta, 1947), pp 47-65, *Ma'athir-ul-Umara*, Vol. I, pp. 578, 835.
27. For Muhammad Azam; *Ma'asir-i-Alamgiri*, pp. 116, 204, for Muhammad Mu'azzam *Ma'asir-i-Alamgiri*, p. 295, *Ma'athir-ul-Umara*, Vol. II, p. 293.

In their case, however, the two princes were probably represented by *naibs* acting on their behalf in the province.

Examples of the intra-regional transfer of *Subadars* are similarly to be found in seventeenth-century Persian chronicles. Said Khan Bahadur was *Subadar* Multan in 1641-42 between his two short terms at Lahore, and was subsequently appointed once again to the Multan *Subadari* in 1645-46.[28] Mukarram Khan Mir Ishaq who served as *Subadar* Multan during the reign of Aurangzeb, had on an earlier occasion been the *Subadar* of Lahore.[29] Conversely, Qulij Khan Turani was made the *Subadar* of Lahore in 1643-44 after he has twice held the *Subadari* of Multan.[30]

Bahadur Khan the *Subadar* of Lahore in 1655-56, too, had been *Subadar* of Multan earlier in 1648-49.[31] Even amongst the *naib-Subadars* we find Syed Abdul Razzaq Gilani who had been Dara Shikoh's deputy in Multan (1654-55 to 1656-57) also served in the same capacity on behalf of Dara Shikoh at Lahore in 1656-57.[32] It is possible that Abdul Razzaq had a familiarity with the region that prompted Dara, to some extent, to depute him to the *naib-subadari* of these *Subas* on both occasions.

From these examples it appears, therefore, that despite the *Subadars* of the province being regularly transferred, their experience and knowledge of the regional pecularities does not seem to have been totally lost to the Mughal Administration once they had been shifted from a particular post. The same appears to have been equally true for other officials of the *Suba* such as the *diwans* and *Bakshis*. We know relatively little about the persons who occupied these offices in Punjab during Mughal times. Nevertheless, from the few references that we come accross it appears likely that these officials were often shifted in the same capacity from one

---

28. *Amal-i-Salih*, Vol. II, pp. 342, 362, 377, 397, 502.
29. *Ma'asir-i-Alamgiri*, p. 173, *Ma'athir-ul-Umara*, Vol. II, p. 244. See also M. Athar Ali, *The Mughal Nobility under Aurangzeb*, p. 227.
30. *Amal-i-Salih*, Vol. II, pp. 4, 10, 397, 431, *Ma'athir-ul-Umara*, Vol. II, p. 543.
31. *Amal-i-Salih*, Vol. III, pp. 65, 239.
32. *Amal-i-Salih*, Vol. III, pp. 215, 266-67, *Ma'athir-ul-Umara*, Vol. II, p. 1079.

place to another within the region of Punjab or returned to the same position after a time gap. For instance, Bihari Mal who served one term as *Diwan* in Lahore in the late 1630s also served a second tenure in the same capacity in Multan in 1638-39.[33] Murshid Quli (Ali Mardan Khan), too, served as the *Diwan* of Lahore during 1639-40 and subsequently held the same office in Multan in 1640-41.[34] Among the Bakshis we know of Muhammad Shafi who was first posted in Lahore during 1619-20 and later in Multan in 1620-21.[35] In so far as officials being reappointed after some time to the same place in their previous capacity is concerned, we have the example of Rai Sabha Chand who was the *Diwan* of *Suba* Lahore on two occasions; once in 1638-39 and for the second time around 1653-54.[36]

Surmising from the limited information that we have noted above, it appears that many of the officials specialized in financial administration. It might, perhaps, even be suggested that persons of rather different natures and capacities were required to manage the basically dissimilar offices of *Subadar* and *Faujdar* on the one hand and *Diwan* and *Bakshi* on the other. While the repeated appointment of persons such as Bihari Mal and Rai Sabha Chand to the office of *Diwan* lends support to this suggestion, there were, nevertheless, other officials who held the office either of *Diwan* or of *Faujdar* with equal case. Dianat Khan who was the *Diwan* of *Suba* Lahore during 1630-31 went in 1631-32 as the *Faujdar, Diwan* and *Amin* of Sirhind.[37] Murshid Quli (Ali Mardan Khan) having served tenures as *Diwan* in Lahore as well as in Multan, was placed in 1645-46 as the *Faujdar* of Kangra and subsequently in 1649-50 we hear of him as the *Bakshi* of *Suba* Lahore.[38] Amanat Khan who is known to have

33. *Amal-i-Salih*, Vol. II, p. 304.
34. *Ibid.*, Vol. II, pp. 316, 339.
35. *Tuzuk-i-Jahangiri*, Vol. II, pp. 87, 191.
36. *Amal-i-Salih*, Vol. II, p. 304, Vol. III, p. 203.
37. *Ma'athir-ul-Umara*, Vol. I, p. 484.
38. *Amal-i-Salih*, Vol. II, pp. 316, 339, Vol. III, p. 124, *Ma'athir-ul-Umara*, Vol. II, p. 304.

officiated as *Qiladar* and possibly *Subadar* of *Suba* Lahore sometime between 1675-76 and 1678 is also believed to have held the post of *Diwan* of that province (though obviously not simultaneous to his occupying the position of *Qiladar* or *Subadar*) for some period between the above-mentioned years.[39] In *Suba* Multan, Sheikh Moosvi Gilani the *Diwan* and *bakhshi* in 1651-52 was later (1656-57) appointed as the *naib-subadar* of Dara Shikoh in the same province.[40]

Whatever the nature of the offices occupied by these *mansabdars* the one probability that definitely emerges from this ordering of available data is that a large number of *mansabdars* continued to remain in the region for a much longer duration than is outwardly suggested by contemporary chronicles on account of their frequent reference to the regular transfer of these *mansabdars*.

Coming to the second aspect of provincial administration which we hope to deal with, namely the office of *Faujdar*, it might be fruitful to examine not only the pattern of the transfer of *Faujdars* but also the specific nature and jurisdiction of this office in Punjab. The purpose of the latter exercise would be to discover the extent to which these *Faujdars* in Punjab were adaptable and adjustable entities, responding both to the exigencies of the situation and the political requirements of the 'bureaucratic' elite that may have dominated the region from time to time.

The exact position and role of the *Faujdar* in the Mughal administrative set-up has had its share of confusion and controversy.[41] Even Abul Fazl's explanation of the functions and jurisdiction of this office is of a general nature and does

---

39. *Ma'athir-ul-Umara*, Vol. I, p. 225.
40. Sheikh Moosvi Gilani is the only instance we have of a person functioning as both *Diwan* and *Bakshi* in Punjab. The normal appointment as *Bakshi* of a *Suba* entailed as additional charge as *waqai nawis*.
41. N.A. Siddiqi; *Land Revenue Administration Under the Mughals* (Bombay, 1970), p. 76. Siddiqi, Perhaps comes nearest to the real situation. He argues that the *Faujdari* was a separate unit under the *Faujdar* and quite distinct from other divisions. The *Faujdari* according to him could comprise a *pargana*, a number of *parganas* and at times even a *sarkar*. U.N.

not clarify the picture to any great extent.[42] Among the *Faujdars* of Punjab more frequently mentioned in our sources are those given the charges of militarily strategic areas and forts. The military significance of these areas and forts was primarily on account of their utility as positions from which the hill chieftains or turbulent tribesmen could be coerced into submissiveness. In *Suba* Lahore the *Faujdari* of Kangra appears to have been of particular significance on this account.[43] The importance that was attached to the fort of Kangra and its environs is apparent from the fact that some of the *Faujdars* of this area were at times close relatives of the *Subadars* of Lahore.[44] Whether the appointments were due to imperial policy or on account of local pressure is difficult to say, but what is beyond doubt is the fact that the simultaneous appointment of the *Subadars'* relatives to these positions was not coincidental. This is made obvious from the fact that the removal of the *Faujdar* of Kangra in such

---

Day; *Mughal Government* (New Delhi, 1970), p. 80, regards the *Faujdar* as the executive head of the *sarkar*. On the other hand, P. Saran, *The Provincial Government of the Mughals 1526-1658* (Allahabad, 1941), p. 89, makes a division and argues that there were two classes of post to which *Faujdars* had been appointed as far back as the reign of Sher Shah. 'First as regular heads of districts or *Sarkars* and secondly on special duty, either in cases of emergency or for purposes of military defence to forts and frontier outposts'.

42. Abul Fazl; *Ain-i-Akbari*, H.S. Jarrett (tr), Jadunath Sarkar (Ed.), Reprint (New Delhi 1978), Vol. II, p. 41-2.
43. Kangra was also known and referred to by such names as *Kohistan-i-Shumali Punjab* and *Kohistan-i-Kangra*. The *faujdar* of Kangra hence is also mentioned as *faujdar-i-Kohdaman* or *faujdar-i-Daman-i-Koh Kangra*. Such references are scattered all over contemporary and later works, for example *Ma'asir-i-Jahangiri*, Vol. II, pp. 6, 209, 378, 425, 458; *Ma'athir-ul-Umara*, Vol. II, p. 81, 365, 575, 778; *Alamgirnama*, Vol. I, p. 217.
44. Khanazad Khan, the *Faujdar* appointed in 1640-41 was the son of Said Khan the *Subadar* of Lahore in 1640-43 (with a break in between as *Subadar* of Multan). Khanjar Khan, the *Faujdar* in 1644-45 was a nephew of Qulij Khan, the *Subadar* of Lahore in 1643-46. Mir Khan the *Faujdar* appointed after the 1658 war of succession was the son of Khalilullah Khan, the *Subadar* of Lahore at this time. See *Amal-i-Salih*, Vol. II, pp. 343, 425; *Ma'athir-ul-Umara*, Vol. II, p. 677; *Alamgirnama*, Vol. I, pp. 217, 908, 917.

cases coincided with the transfer of the related *Subadar* of Lahore.[45] A contemporary observer in fact, puts this beyond doubt by making an explicit statement to the effect that because Qulij Khan was the *Subadar* of Punjab (Lahore) at a particular time, his nephew Khanjar Khan was appointed to the *Faujdari* of Kangra.[46]

It is also possible that familial association of some *Faujdars* with the Lahore *Subadars* might have resulted in the former being entrusted with the administration of a larger area. Khanazad Khan and Mir Khan (who held *Faujdaris* at the same time as their fathers were *Subadars* of Lahore, were appointed to the *Faujdari* not only of Khangra, but of Jammu as well. The former was appointed in 1640-41 and the latter immediately after the 1658 war of succession.[47] This nevertheless, only remains a possibility, for on the other hand we have at least simultaneously without being personally related to the *Subadar* of Lahore.[48] On account of the geographical proximity of Kangra and Jammu, it is possible that both these areas were occasionally administered jointly by one person in the subsequent period as well.

In so far as the personal status of the Kangra *Faujdar* was concerned, the largest *mansab* as *Faujdar* of Kangra Jammu about which we have definite information, was that the 3500/3000 held by Mir Khan.[49] Our information regarding the *mansab* holdings of the *Faujdars* of Kangra is, however,

---

45. Both Khanazad Khan and Said Khan, the *Faujdar* and *Subadar* respectively, were removed from their offices in 1642-43. The same seems to have been the case with Khanjar Khan and Qulij Khan in 1645-46. See *Amal-i-Salih*, Vol. II, p. 318, 377, 397, 425, 470.
46. *Ibid.*, Vol. II, p. 425.
47. *Ibid.*, Vol. II, p. 343. See also *Alamgirnama*, Vol. I, pp. 217, 908, 917, *Ma'athir-ul-Umara*, Vol. II, p. 677.
48. This is the instance of Iraj Khan who as *Faujdar* in 1649-50 held this dual charge of Kangra and Jammu at a time when the *Suba* of Lahore was held by Dara Shikoh. See *Ma'athir-i-Umara*, Vol. I, p. 685.
49. *Alamgirnama*, Vol. I, p. 917. It is possible that Najabat Khan who was the *Faujdar* in 1642-43 held a higher *mansab* on account of the fact that he had, in 1638-39, already attained the rank of 4000/4000 as *Subadar* of Multan. We do not, however, have any definite information to suggest that he was appointed as the *Faujdar* of Kangra with the same *mansab*.

extremely meagre. From whatever little we know it seems likely that few of them would have been less than 2000 *zat*, with many of them being 3000 zat.[50] On the other hand, the *Faujdars* who were in charge of merely the *Faujdari* of Jammu did not rank so high in the *mansabdari* hierarchy, and appear to have been *mansabdars* of 1500 to 1000 zat.[51]

Since the *Faujdaris* of Kangra and Jammu were of strategic importance to the Mughal empire, there is reason to believe that *mansabdars* appointed to them were provided with increased support to enable them to perform their duties effectively. This was most appropriately done by granting them conditional *mashrut mansabs*; meaning an increased *mansab* that was to be held by an official for the duration of his appointment to a particular office.[52]

Contemporary chronicles provide virtually no information regarding even the regular *mansabs* of appointees to *Faujdaris* much less could possible be learnt from them about the details of the *Faujdars'mashrut* holdings. We do, nevertheless, have the instance of Mukarram Khan, the *Subadar* of Lahore, (1695) who held a *mashrut* rank of 300 *sawar* for being in charge of the *Faujdari* of Jammu apart from his *Subadari*. This conditional rank was withdrawn when the *Faujdari* was transferred from

---

50. This information is tabulated in my unpublished Ph.D. thesis, 'Socio-Economic Conditions in Punjab During the 17th Century', approved by the Centre for Historical Studies, Jawaharlal Nehru University, New Delhi. Between 1612 and 1671 we have so far learnt of twenty-two *Faujdars* being appointed in Kangra.
51. From available source material we know of only two cases of *Faujdars* of Jammu with higher *mansabs*. They were Qawam-ud-din Khan the *Subadar* of Lahore from 1678-79 to 1680-81, who was also given the additional charge of the *Faujdari* of Jammu and Mukarram Khan, *Subadar* Lahore in 1695, who was also *Faujdar* Jammu for some time. See *Ma'asir-i-Alamgiri*, pp. 103, 235. *Akbarat* (Sitamau Transcripts), 38th Regnal Year, Aurangzeb, dated 23rd Shawwal. Here again the *mansabdars* in question were not really *Faujdars* of Jammu alone, but also held other important charges at the *Suba* headquarters.
52. For a more elaborate explanation refer M. Athar Ali; *The Mughal Nobility Under Aurangzeb*, pp. 41-2. When the *mansabdar* was no longer in charge of a post requiring a *mashrut mansab*, he was to be reverted to the original *mansab* he had held prior to his appointment to the post.

his charge.[53] From a document of Aurangzeb's region, we also learn about Munim Khan, the *Faujdar* of Jammu who was also the *Naib-subadar* of Lahore (1706-07) having a *mansab* of 1500/1000 of which 500/600 were conditional.[54]

It might also be mentioned that Kangra was among the few *Faujdaris* in Punjab where apart from the *Faujdar*, specific mention is also made to the appointment of a *qila dar* to the fort of Kangra.[55] This reference by contemporary sources to be *Qila'dar* of Kangra may not be merely an exercise in detail when we realize after the scrutiny of the available material that the *mansab* ranking of the *Qila'dar* of Kangra may frequently have been higher than that of the *Qila'dar* of Lahore.[56] This difference in status can, perhaps be explained

53. *Akbarat*, (Sitamau Transcripts), 38th Regnal year, Aurangzeb, dated 23rd Shawwal, corresponding to 27 May 1695m, p. 467.
54. *Ibid.*, 51st Regnal year, Aurangzeb, *Sha'aban*, p. 175. Munim Khan being the *Diwan* of Prince Muhammad Muazzam held a *mashrut* rank of too *sawar* on that account. That much of his conditional rank was because of the *Faujdari* of Jammu becomes clear from the statement in this document that in Ja. 1707 '500/100 out of his conditional *mansab* for the *Faujdari* of Jammu was made unconditional'. We see that the entire increase in his *zat* was derived from his holding the office of *Faujdar*.
55. Quite possibly, many of the forts of the other *Faujdars* had regularly appointed qiladars. The Qiladar of Kangra fort is referred to due to the prominence of the fort, and the importance that had been attached to its capture during the reign of Jahangir. Another place where reference is made to the appointment of a *Qiladar* is Attock, which was a kind of frontier post for the Mughals and a strict vigilance was kept on people crossing the river at this place. Dawar Dad is known to have been both *Faujdar* and *Qiladar* of Attock immediately after the 1658 war of succession, and in 1685 when *Bakhshi* Abul Fatah Khan was the *Faujdar* of Attock, we are told that the *Qiladari* was held by someone else. *A descriptive List of Vakil Reports addressed to the Rulers of Jaipur*, Vol. I (Persian) (Rajasthan State Archives, Bikaner, 1967), p. 15, Serial No. 81.
56. Yusuf Aqa, *Qiladar* of Lahore in 1650-51 was *mansabdar* of 1000/400, Amanullah Khan *Qilddar* in 1658-59 held 1000/200, and Amanat Khan the *Qiladar* of Lahore sometime between 1675-76 and 1678 held 1000/200 till 1678. On the other hand the *Qiladars* of Kangra held *mansabs* as follows:
Alf Khan Qiyamkhani 1620-21 1500/1000.
Safi Khan 1656-57 2000/1000.
Raja Mandhata 1670-71 1000/1000.

(Contd. to next page)

by the presence of the *Subadar* and his large garrison at Lahore, which would enable the *Qila'dar* to draw upon it if such a need arose. The *Qila'dar* of Kangra on the other hand, on account of his distance from the *Suba* headquarters and the possibility of the frequent absence of the *Faujdar* from Kangra due to law and order duties, would have to be more self-reliant and might be called upon to defened the fort with only the force he had at his personal command. Hence the need for a large *mansab*.

As in the case of the officials at the *Suba* headquarters (*Subadar, Diwan* etc.) the transfer of *Faujdars* too, took place quite frequently within the region itself. Among the *Faujdars* of Kangra, therefore, are to be gound names of *mansabdars* who occupied other official positions within Punjab, either before or after their tenure in Kangra. Najabat Khan who seems to have been *Faujdar* of Kangra on two occasions (1630-31 to 1634-35 and 1642-43) had earlier been *naib-subadar* of Multan in 1630-31 and the full fledged *Subadar* of that province from 1638-39 to 1640-41.[57] Similarly Murshid Quli (Ali Mardan Khan) the *Faujdar* in 1645-46 had previously served as the *Diwan* of *Suba* Lahore (1639-40) and Suba Multan (1640-41).[58] It is perhaps due to their familiarity with the region that these officials continued to be appointed to offices and areas located within Punjab. To the *Faujdari* of Kangra were even appointed *mansabdars* who belonged to areas that lay within the Faujdari jurisdiction itself; *mansabdars* like Raja Suraj Mal and Rajrup.[59]

Another important *Faujdari* which was, in nature, very similar to that of Kangra was the *Faujdari* of Lakhi Jangal in

(Contd. from previous page)

See *Amal-Salih*, Vol. III, pp. 138, 248, *Alamgirnama*, Vol. I, pp. 197, 296; *Ma'athir-ul-Umara*, Vol. p. 225 and Vol. III, p. 668; *Ma'asir-i-Jahangiri*, p. 318, *Tuzuk-i-Jahangiri*, Vol. II, p. 283. J.S. Grewal, 'Some Persian Documents From Nurpur', in *Miscellaneous Articles* (Amritsar, 1974), pp. 34-6.

57. *Amal-i-Salih*, Vol. IIN, pp. 6, 308, 318; *Ma'athir-ul-Umara*, Vol. II, pp. 81, 365-6.
58. *Amal-i-Salih*, Vol. II, pp. 316, 339, 428, *Ma'athir-ul-Umara*, Vol. II, p. 304.
59. *Ma'asir-i-Jahangiri*, pp. 197, 246, *Ma'athir-ul-Umara*, Vol. II, p. 304.

the *Suba* of Multan.[60] Though it contained some well settled agricultural areas, there were also to be found within the jurisdiction of this *Faujdari*, some turbulent tribal elements.[61] The suppression of these elements, hence was an important duty of the *Faujdars* of this region and *mansabdars* appointed there were, probably required, to be men of sufficient military experience. Concluding from the limited information that we have with us, it seems that the person to be appointed as *Faujdar* of Lakhi jangal with the highest *mansab* (10,000 zat) was Prince Muhammad Mu'izz-ud-din, the son of Muhammad Mu'azzam, towards the latter part of Aurangzeb's region. The highest *mansab* held by a noble as *Faujdar* of Dipalpur-Lakhi Jangal was, probably, that of 4000/4000 by Mubariz Khan in 1644-45.[62] Towards the end of the seventeenth century, this *Faujdari* assumed greater importance due to the increased tribal unrest it witnessed. The appointment of Prince Muhammad Mu'izz-ud-din as *Faujdar* in order to supress this unrest, testifies to the significance it had in the eyes of Aurangazeb.[63]

Though Lakhi Jangal was usually held by *Faujdars* as a separate charge, there were occasion when it was territorially combined with the areas of some other *Faujdaris*. Todar Mal (Afzal Khan), as we shall see later, was appointed to a charge that included not only Dipalpur but also Sirhind, Jalandhar, and Sultanpur. Two other exceptions of this nature can be seen in the cases of Sardar Khan who was the *Faujdar* of both Lakhi

---

60. Though the *Faujdari* was called Lakhi Jangal it appears that the headquarters of the *Faujdari* were located in Dipalpur. For the mapping of this area refer Irfan Habib; *As Atlas of the Mughal Empire* (Delhi, 1982). Plate 4a. Therefore, those *mansabdars* mentioned as *faujdars* of Dipalpur were also, probably, *Faujdars* of Lahi Jangal and vice-versa.
61. Sujan Rai Bhandari, *Khulasat-ul-Tawarikh*, M. Zafar Hasan (Ed.) (Delhi, 1918), p. 63. The tribes mentioned are the Dogars, Wattus and Gujars. See also *Asrar-i-Samadi*, M. Shujauddin (Ed.), Research Society of Pakistan (Lahore, 1965), p. 9. Reference here is made to the Battis, Kharsal and Dogars.
62. This rank was attained by him in 1637-38 and in the normal course he was likely to have held the same rank in 1641-45 or even been promoted to a higher one. *Amal-i-Salih*, Vol. II, p. 411, *Ma'athir-ul-Umara*, Vol. II, p. 105.
63. *Ruka'at-i-Alamgiri*; Jamashid, II, Bilmoria (tr), reprint (Delhi, 1972), p. 75.

jangal and Tihara in 1634-35, and Khawwas Khan who succeeded him to his dual charge in the same year and probably held it until the year 1640-41.[64] The jurisdiction of the *Faujdari* in the last two cases, therefore, included territory from *Suba* Multan as well as *Suba* Delhi.[65]

Such flexibility in territorial jurisdiction was apparently a normal feature of *Faujdaris* in Punjab. Most of the other *Faujdaris* that find mentions in our sources were not of the same military significance as Kangra and Lakhi Jangal. They were probably created for ensuring the collection of revenue from the more powerful assessees and for the maintenance of law and order. The information derived from references to these *Faujdaris* is of an insignificant nature and does not add very much to our understanding about them.[66] A few *Faujdaris*, however, are referred to in some what greater detail, and it is from these references that we learn about the flexible nature of their boundaries.

Sometimes a *Faujdari* was held as a separate charge by an appointee while at other times two *Faujdari* areas were combined and controlled by one person. Yosuf Chelah, the *Faujdar* of Eminabad in 1655-56 who was transferred to Sialkot in the same year, held these *Faujdaris* as separate and independent charges.[67] So was the case with Mir Ahmad Khan at Eminabad during Aurangzeb's region and with Ganga Dhar the *Faujdar* of Sialkot in 1653-54.[68] On the other hand, Irabat Khan (Azam Kham Mir Muhammad Baqir) had during the reign of Jahangir, held the *Faujdari* of both Sialkot and Gujarat

64. *Amal-i-Salih*, Vol. II, p. 296; *Ma'athir-ul-Umara*, Vol. I, p. 826.
65. See Irfan Habib; *An Atlas of the Mughal Empire*, Plate 4A.
66. Some *Faujdaris* mentioned only in passing are those of Mung, Rasulpur and the areas between Jandals and Lahore. See *Akbarnama*, Vol. IIIm, p. 921. Mention is made here of the appointment of *Faujdars* to these areas in order to control the *zamindars*. We learn about the existence of the *Faujdaris* of Bhera and Khushab, Nurmahal and Sultanpur from other contemporary sources. There must have been numerous other *Faujdars* in Punjab that came into existence or were abolished during the course of the 17th century.
67. *Amal-i-Salih*, Vol. II, p. 220.
68. *Ma'athir-ul-Umara*, Vol. I, p. 160; *Amal-i-Salih*, Vol. III, p. 203.

simultaneously.[69] We also learn elsewhere that Firoz Rustom Khan a *mansabdar* of Aurangazeb's region was entrusted with the enlarged *Faujdari* of Changab-Ravi Doab.[70] Another dual charge of a different nature is seem from the case of Rai Sabha Chand the *Diwan* of Punjab who was also appointed simultaneously as the *Faujdar* of Sialkot.[71] Similarly even the *Faujdari* of Jalandhar while sometimes held as a seperate charge was on occasions combined with the *Faujdari* of Sirhind.

While Kangra and Lakhi Jangal provide us with typical examples of military *Faujdaris*, Sirhand represents on which was essentially created for revenue purpose. A glance at the *mansabdars* appointed to Sirhind reveals them as being quite obviously more familiar with revenue administration than with military work. Raj Kashi Das, Dianat Khan and Todar Mal (Afzal Khan) were among the persons we know as having been in charge of the *Faujdari* of Sirhind. Most of the area under the jurisdiction of this *Faujdari*, was probably, constituted by zamindaris which paid their land revenue regularly and hence required the *Faujdar* to maintain only a small military force. The *mansab* rank of some *Faujdars* of Sirhind, despite the large area they controlled was possibly for this reason lower than the *mansab* held by many other

---

69. Farid Bhakkari, *Dhakhirat-al-Khawanin*, Syed Moinul Haq (Ed.), Pakistan Historical Society, 3 Vols. Vol. I, 1961, Vol. II, 1970, Vol. III, 1974. See Vol. II, p. 200; *Ma'athir-ul-Umara*, Vol. I, p. 315. Sialkot Gujarat are located on opposite banks of the river *Chenab* and speaking strictly in terms of *sarkar* jurisdiction, were parts of different *sarkars*.
70. *Alamgirnama*, Vol. II, p. 216. This appears to be a very large area and included both Sialkot and Eminabad, which are also mentioned in some cases as being separate *Faujdaris*. In this case, however, they seem to have been combined in order to constitute one single *Faujdari*. The jurisdiction of this *Faujdari* apparently coincided with the entire *sarkar*.
71. *Ibid.*, Vol. III, p. 203. The association of the diwan with a *faujdari* in this region may also perhaps, be seen in the light of the fact that this *Faujdari* area's revenue was probably allotted to the maintenance of the Kabul soldiers. This was the case at least in the early years of Bahadur Shah's reign. See *Akbarat*, (Sitamau Transcripts), Bahadur Shah, 5th Regnal year, Vol. II, pp. 399, 439-40, 459.

Faujdars.[72] The designation used for the official in charge of Sirhind is frequently that of *Diwan*, *Amin* and *Faujdar.*[73] It appears, in fact, that the function entailed by the first two charges was of greater importance in Sirhind than that of its *Faujdari*.

Todar Mal (Afzal Khani) appears to have been the most prominent of the *mansabdars* in charge of Sirhind. Starting as *Diwan*, *Amin* and *Faujdar* or Sirhind in 1639-40, he was in 1640-41, also given the *Faujdari* of Lakhi Jangal. Later in 1647-48 we learn that Todar Mal was the *Diwan*, amin and *Faujdar* of Sirhind, Dipalpur, Jalandhar and Sultanpur and until 1658 was at any rate the *Faujdar* at least of Sirhind, if not of the whole area.[74] From this it becomes apparent that the territory of which Todar Mal was appointed included areas not only from different *sarkars*, such as Sirhind, Between Jalandhar and Dipalpur, but also three *Subas*, viz. Delhi, Lahore and Multan.

The primary reason for giving Todar Mal the control of such a large area seems to be his success in extending agricultural and in populating the *Khalisa* lands of this region.[75] It is, therefore, likely that he was associated primarily with revenue and finance, while being militarily

---

72. This has been tabulated in my Ph.D. thesis, Socio-Economic Conditions in *Punjab* during the 17th Century', In brief may be mentioned here the *mansab* holding of some of the *Faujdars* of Sirhind. Dianat Khan (1631-32) 1000/400, Shaikh Abdul Karim (during the war of succession)2000/1000, Abdul Nabi Khan 1500/1500 Baqir Khan (1661) 1000/1000, Abdul Aziz (1664-65) 1500/700.
73. There are also some other terms used for the mansabdar in charge of Sirhind. Abdul Karim is mentioned as being the thanedar and mutassaddi of Sirhind and at a later date Abdul Nabi is referred to as the *nazim*. *Khulasat-ul-Tawarikh*, p. 525; *Alamgirnama*, Vol. I, p. 443. We also have the instance of Yusuf Chelab being appointed in the *faujdari* and aminin first of Eminabad and later of Sialkot. See *Amal-i-Salih*, Vol. III, p. 220. This may have been the designation of some other *faujdars* as well, but it is only with regard to Sirhind that it is most frequently and explicitly mentioned in our sources.
74. See *Amal-i-Salih*, Vol. II, pp. 330, 342, 578, 459; Vol. III, p. 7; *Khulasat-ul-Tawarikh*, p. 525; *Ma'athir-ul-Umara*, Vol. II, p. 958.
75. *Amal-i-Salih*, Vol. II, p. 345.

aided by other imperial officials who provided him with additional support in areas where it was required. This possibility is further substantiated by the fact that his *mansab* rank, though highest among the *Faujdars* appointed to Sirhind, was not really commensurate with the vast extent of the area that was put under his charge.[76] This disparity suggests that his control over the area was more in the nature of a *Diwan* or *Amin* over the revenue administration and much less as a *Faujdar* over his *Faujdari*.[77]

From this brief survey it appears that the *Faujdaris* in Punjab did not constitute rigid territorial jurisdictions, and were often combined or separated from time to time. It is quite likely, however, that apart from administrative requirements, the personal influence of the *mansabdar* concerned may have much to do with the manner in which *Faujdaris* were reorganised. Even the nature of these *Faujdaris* varied. While some were military in nature many others were created basically for revenue purposes. Expressive of the adaptiveness of Mughal local administration is the case of the *Faujdari* of Sirhind under Todar Mal, where we find areas from both kinds of *Faujdaris*. It may not be entirely wrong to say, therefore, that in the seventeenth century the nature and jurisdiction of *Faujdaris* could hardly conformed to a rigid and preconceived political or administrative framework. Much

76. In 1642-43 when Todar Mal was in charge of the *Faujdari* of both Sirhind and Lakhi Jangal, his *mansab* stood at 1000/1000 (2 - 3h) and in 1646-47 was further increased by 300 *suwar* (2-3*h*).In 1647-48 his mansab stood at 2000/2000. Though this large *suwar* rank may have enabled him to meet to some extent his requirements military support, he could not possibly have covered effectively the entire area on his own.

77. This difference in the nature of control can be compared with instances of *Faujdars* who had effective military control over their territories. The military significance of Lakhi Jangal has already been pointed out, as also the importance of some of its *faujdars*. Some of them while holding Lakhi Jangal as a single charge had fairly large *mansabs*. Asad Khan (1628-29 to 1630-31) had 2500/2500, Sazawar Khan (1632-33 to 1634-35) had 2500/2000, Dindar Khan (1664-65) had 2500/2000, Prince Muhammad Mu'iziz-ud-din had 10,000 zat. On the other hand Todar Mal who was given charge of a larger area, had in 1647-48*a mansab* of only 2000/2000. Tabulated in my Ph.D., thesis, 'Socio-Economic Conditions in Punjab during the 17th Century'.

seems to have depended on local conditions even though the formal authority for undertaking the necessary adaptations seems to have originated from the imperial government.

Quite apparently the authority and power of the Mughal Emperor to order the transfer of *mansabdars* in the province and to alter the administrative boundaries of territorial units seems to have been undisputed. That this authority was not exercised without certain socio-political constraints is also, however, to an extent, borne out by some of the observations made above. The appointment of influential nobles belonging to the region as *Subadars* or *Faujdars* may not have been entirely on account of a passing whim of the Emperor. In fact, there exists the strong possibility that political considerations almost necessitated such appointments. Moreover, it may be rather difficult to separate from the causes, the consequences of influential nobles remaining officially positioned in a province for a long duration. Many of them were likely to have developed powerful vested interests that could best be protected by remaining in the region, and which would become even more firmly entrenched by their continued residence in or official control over the area. This regionalisation of the administrative functionaries even at the level of *Diwans, Bakshis* and *Faujdars* seems to suggest that while the Mughal Empire may outwardly appear to have been highly centralised on account of its elaborate procedures if governance and formal monopoly over the instruments of effective political control, the regional diversity of the empire could hardly be accommodated within a rigid and centralised 'bureaucratic' framework. Essential for the survival of the Empire was its ability to incorporate the regional landed elite as well as to create an administrative one. It is possible that the mingling of the two would encourage the emergence of a force whose existence and influence was not entirely derived from central authority.

To carry the argument further, it might be suggested that administrative requirements and pressure goups of a local and regional nature were important enough to prompt deviations from what have widely come to be regarded as some of the fundamental principles of Mughal administration.

Among these principles were the procedures regarding the transfer of officials and explicit division of territorial and functional jurisdictions so as to avoid the emergence of powerful local interests. Such being the case, it might be asked whether Abul Fazl's observations on these principles are not merely elaborations of an ideal situation or structure that may never have existed in any substantial manner.

It is possible that the subsequent developments in eighteenth century Punjab have origins traceable to our period of study to the long term emergence of a regional administrative elite. This elite was one that, perhaps, came into existence in opposition to established Mughal Policy and elite that was encouraged (unwittingly or otherwise) in practice. Indeed, the high degree of Mughal centralization, so commonly an assumption among medievalists, might yet turn out to be an illusion.

4

FORMATION OF DIMASA STATE IN MEDIEVAL NORTH EAST INDIA

J.B. Bhattacharjee

THE state as an ancient institution, is a specific kind of social organisation which "gives expression to the existing relations in a society and to ideas pertaining to power, authority, force, justice, property and many other phenomena".[1] Radcliffe-Brown considered it as "a collection of individual human beings connected by a complex system of relations".[2] The unique type of relations between the various communities which are possible only by social stratification and class division, could be perpetuated through several stages of development. As Engels puts it.[3] "The state has not existed from all eternity. There have been societies which have managed without it, which had no notion of the state or state power. At a definite stage of economic development, which necessarily involved the cleavage of society into classes, the state became a necessity because of this cleavage".

1. Henry J.M., Claessen and Peter Skalnik; (ed.) *The Early State*, Mouton Publishers, The Hague, 1978, p. 4.
2. A.R. Radcliffe-Brown; *"Preface"* in M. Fortes & E.E. Evans-Pitchard (ed.), *African Political Systems*, London, 1940, p. XIII.
3. Friedrich, Engels; *The Origin of the family, private property and the state*, London, 1972, p. 232.

The States so characterized are, however, of two distinct categories, viz. (*i*) Modern, and (*ii*) Early, the division being based on the stages of development that the societies have passed through as a historical process. The Modern States are complex, industrialized and developing, while the Early States are simple, non-industrialized and precapitalistic. The studies on the process of state formation as a distinct area of interest of the Social Scientists refer to the Early State and they mostly cover the states that emerged from egalitarian tribal bases. Although early in content, those precapitalistic formations which incorporated considerable feudalistic elements of regional types might be as late a phenomena as in this century.

In the Indian context this area of study becomes all the more fascinating due to the twin processes of cultural assimilation and economic interaction, although the state or polity formations that emerged from the indigenous tribal bases in precolonial India continues to be an area less explored by the social Scientists.[4]

This paper is an attempt at an understanding of the governing factors of Dimasa State formation in Cachar and its structural characteristics, on the basis of the conceptual frame that emerges from contemporary researches and the empirical data that have been drawn from conventional historical sources.

---

4. Surajit Sinha, *"State Formation and Rajput Myth in Tribal Central India"*, *Man in India*, Vol. 42, No.1, January-March, 1962, pp. 35-80.
It was Dr. Surajit C. Sinha who, in his Presidential Address to the Anthropology and Archaeology section of the forty-ninth session of the Indian Science Congress at Cuttack in 1962, had for the first time referred to this significant field of research and suggested the hypotheses and methods for study of state formation among the tribes of central India on the basis of his own research. Sinha's pioneering contribution inspired further investigation in this aspect of tribal traditions, relying primarily on historical data. Hermam Kulke of the University of Berne, for example, has done excellent work on the Orissa region. Under Sinha's leadership again the Centre for Studies in Social Sciences, Calcutta, sponsored a project in 1980 on "Tribal Politics and State Systems in Pre-colonial Eastern and North-Eastern India" which covered the *Ahom* state, *Cachar, Manipur, Jaintia, Khasi States* and the *Mizos* from the North-east. Hermann Kulke, *"Early State formation and Royal Legitimation in Tribal Areas of Eastern India"*, Cf. R.R. Moser & M.K. Gautam (ed.), *Aspects of Tribal Life in South Asia I, Strategy and Survivals*, Bernensia, 1978.

The Conceptual Frame[5]

Our researches in tribal state and polity formations in medieval India suggest that there had been some common elements in the process of such formations in all cases, although some of these elements, and not others, might have been more prominent in specific cases. These include: (*i*) the tribal formations underwent transformation with the emergence of private property, when the tribal societies were stratified into classes in terms of differentiated land-holding

---

5. This section is reproduced from my paper "Tripuri State Formation in Medieval Tripura", *Proceedings of the North East India History Association,* Third Session, 1982, pp. 67-72, Wherein the frame was drawn from, besides the works of Sinha and Kulke cited above, the contributions of Amalendu Guha *(Ahom state)*, Barun De (Concepts and Issues) and my own note (*Dimasa State*) in an workshop organised by the CSSS, Calcutta, in July 1981.
I had concluded my paper on *'Tripuri State'* in following words:
"I study of the history of the Tripuri state formation reveals the factors and process and processes that helped the elevation of the political system from a tribal base to a well developed monarchy. The leadership of the tribe had passed into the hands of a single personality on hereditary line during the migrations and attempts at establishing a principality of their own. The initial settlement in the wet rice cultivation area predominated by the Indo-Aryan Bengalees exposed the tribe to Hindu influences that resulted in social stratification and ligitimisation of the status of the ruler by the Brahmins who testified the divine origin of the royal clan and thereby enlisted the loyalty of the people. The military support received from the neighbouring larger state of Bengal enabled the ruler to overcome any possible opposition to his assumed authority and to subdue the bordering hill tribes and in extending the boundary of the state. The leadership in war against neighbouring imperial forces and warlike chieftains strengthened his position further and helped to develop an adequate defence system. The protective position of the ruler and his universalized social status helped in organising an elaborate hierarchical order suitable without any opposition from the members of his tribe or indigenous population. The support and loyalty of the more productive non tribals were enforced by the Raja's projected role as the champion of his new faith and their cultural and lingustic assimilation with the majority group in the state. The sustenance came in the form of surplus extraction in terms of tirbute and taxes and personal service and the Rajas themselves indulging in profitable trades".

and the extent of political dominance that strengthened the position of the traditional chiefs at clan/tribe level; (*ii*) the sphere of political dominance of a chief was extended either by subduing the neighbouring tribes/ clans/communities or by direct territorial conquest or by their voluntary submission to his protective authority; (*iii*) the authority was further strengthened by leading the people in war path either for offensive or for defensive purposes and it continued to be unquestioned, at least at the formative stage, in cases where the state came into existence through military adventurism; (*iv*) the ruling chiefs succeeded in developing a centralised administration with an elaborate defense structure and the means to appropriate surplus through a hierarchical state order; (*v*) the introduction of more developed agricultural technology to ensure increased production, and the production control on the part of the ruler could be an essential precondition for a centralised state authority; (*vi*) the families with traditions of administrative proficiency and artisans and peasants were induced to immigrate and settle in the territory; (*vii*) the process of Hinduisation/Sanskritisation and the role of the Brahmins in establishing the divine origin of the ruler helped the legitimization of the assumed status of the latter and its consolidation, and the myths that were created in the process resulted in the universalisation of the culture; (*viii*) the adoption of the language and culture of the majority in the territory's population by the ruling family and the aristocracy enlisted loyalty and support of that dominant revenue-paying group; (*ix*) the rulers emerged as the champions of their new faith and patrons of the culture and language of their subjects; (*x*) the matrimonial connections with the ruling houses in other states, with almost similar ethno-cultural traditions evoked mutual support and raised them in the estimation of their subjects; and (*xi*) the diplomatic relations with more powerful neighbours were essential either to guarantee political existence in the face of expanding influences of such neighbours or to pacify the disgruntled elements within the state.

The Early State Model

A recent publication, entitled *The Early State*[6], which includes twenty-one case studies covering all the major regions of the globe suggests that (*i*) the population growth and population pressure, (*ii*) war, the threat of war or conquest, raids, (*iii*) conquest, (*iv*) progress in production and the promotion of a surplus, tribute, affluence, (*v*) ideology and legitimation, and (*vi*) the influence of already existing states, are the major factors that inspired the development into statehood in most cases.

The volume includes a case study of the Kachari (*Dimasa*) State[7] by Sofia A. Maretina of the Academy of Sciences, Leningrad, USSR, which although based on insufficient empirical data (the report of a British officer of Haflong in 1885)[8] being the only historical document used by the author successfully brings out that the development of the *Dimasa* social organisation into unique statehood was triggered by the elements that are by and large common in twenty other cases in the volume. In his classification of these cases into *inchoate* (dominant kinship ties), *typical* (kinship ties counterbalances by ties of locality) and *transitional* (administrative apparatus dominated by appointed officials) types, Claessen[9] puts the Kachari State in the typical cluster, complaining, of course, that the data supplied by Maretina was not sufficient.[10] He also admitted the inadequacy of Maretina's data by showing that for "Structural Comparisons" of the twenty-one listed cases no data was available to him on crucial items like sacral status of the sovereign, sovereign as law giver, sovereign as protector, sovereign presents gifts to the people, sovereign remunerates his people for services rendered, sovereign pays

---

6. Claessen & Skalnik, N.I.
7 *Ibid.*, pp. 339-358.
8. C.A. Soppitt, *An historical and descriptive account of the Kachari tribes in the North Cachar Hills*, Shillong, 1885.
9. Henry J.M. Claessen, "The Early State: A Structural Approach", N. 1, pp. 589-593.
10. *Ibid.*, p. 591.

offerings, heads of certain clans belong to aristocracy, anonymous functionaries, courtiers exercise influence on political affairs, influence of priest in decision making, serveillance apparatus, etc.[11] She could find some data only on trade and markets, social stratification, informal influence on law giving commoners obligations to perform manual services for the state and aristocracy, differentiation between the upper and the lower strata, formal judiciary etc.[12] But in Peter Skalnik's penaltimate chapter, "the Early State as a Process"[13], based on the same case studies there is no reference to the Kachari State at all. In the concluding chapter, entitled "Limits: Beginning and End of the Early State", Claessen and Skalnik noticed that in the Kachari case the population growth stimulated the growth of extended families, in which the social distance between senior and junior lineages become unbridgeable.[14] They also noticed that wars and raids contributed to the emergence of stronger leaders and a better and stronger organisations, be it for purposes of defense or offence,[15] and the influence of already existing state systems in Kachari organisation.[16] Although in the chapter on "Structural Approach" Claessen listed the Kachari State in his group of *typical* states in a section in the concluding chapter that deals with the *inchoate* states after discussing the characteristics of the *inchoate* states, the authors observed that the same situation most probably prevailed in the Kachari State (among others). "Where groups of subjugated people were joined to the original population core".[17] They had nothing to mention about the Kachari State in the section on the 'End of the Early State',[18] while about the 'Origin of the Early State' they said,[19] "The Kachari state

11. *Ibid.*, pp. 537-588.
12. *Ibid.*
13. *Ibid.*, pp. 597-618.
14. *Ibid.*, p. 625.
15. *Ibid.*, p. 626.
16. *Ibid.*, p. 629.
17. *Ibid.*, p. 532.
18. *Ibid.*, pp. 633-634.
19. *Ibid.*, p. 623.

originated in the hill districts of the northeastern part of the Indian subcontinent. Even before the state came into being, a disintegration of the clan system had occurred. The genealogical group gradually made way for a socio-professional type of group, which initiated growing social inequality. As the population grew the number of these groups also grew. Incessant warfare consolidated the position of the notables. The influence of military leaders was considerable. Technical as well as socio-political concepts were borrowed from surrounding states; these had a substantial impact upon the formation of the Kachari State".

Claessen and Skalnik's *The Early State* is an excellent addition to the existing literature in this emerging area of interest to social Scientists. In fact, it is perhaps the only work in which the leading theories and hypotheses on state formation have been tested on the basis of a large number of case studies in a global context. It is unfortunate, as the learned editors themselves have repeatedly admitted, that they were not posted with enough data, sufficient for an understanding of the process of formation, the characteristics and the causes of decline of the *Dimasa* State.

It should, however, be said in favour of Maretina that she could build up an excellent case study on the basis of extremely scanty data at her command and that her basis assumptions and conclusions remain valid inspite of additional and more authenticated historical evidences that one is able to cite, primarily due to her strong theoretical base and a sound understanding of the historical and sociological process. This further justifies that certain elements are bound to be common in the process of precapitalistic early state formations as enunciated in our conceptual frame for studies in the tribal state formations in precolonial India. In her conclusion, Maretina lists the following specific characteristics of the formations of primitive state-like unions in Northeast India.[20]

(1) The slow rate and due to short period of the existence of the state like unions of this type, the

20. *Ibid.*, p. 357.

incompleteness of the process of class formation in early states. Hence the preclass (or early class) character of these states.

(2) The basic preservation of traces of the clan structure in the hierarchy of the social strata.

(3) The importance of the role played by war in the stabilization of states and in the strengthening of the dominant position of privileged social strata.

(4) The indispensability of contacts with advanced state systems to provide the required attributes of a state structure.

(5) The greater role played by the ecological factor than in the case of more advanced stages of development, as reflected in the difference in evolution between the hill areas and the plains.

(6) The transfer to the plains as an indispensable factor in the formation of the early state.

We shall trace in the following pages the history of the Dimasa State formation on the basis of conventional data, independent of Maretina's study.

The Dimasa Case

Cachar or *Hreamba-rajya* that was integrated in the British Colonial empire in India in three instalments in 1832, 1835 and 1854 on the eve of British annexation included besides Cachar and North Cachar Hills districts of Assam, the parts of Nowgong (Hojai Davaka area) in Assam, Dayung-Dhansiri valley in Nagaland and the Jui Frontier Area in Manipur.[21] The state had three distinct administrative divisions, designated on geographical basis, *viz.* South (Cachar plains) North (hills division) and Central (Nowgong Section).[22] The ethnic character of the divisions also varied as the south Cachar was peopled mainly by the Bengalees, North by the *Dimasas*, and the Central by *Dimasa*, Karbi, Hojai, Lalung etc. tribes.

---

21. J.B. Bhattacharjee, *Cachar Under British Rule in North East India*, New Delhi, 1977, P. 1, F. Hamilton, An Account of Assam, London, 1820, p. 83.
22. W. Robinson; *A Descriptive Account of Assam*, Calcutta, 1841m p. 399.

The ruling tribe of the state was *Dimasa* which belonged to the Bodo family of the Tibeto-Burman race of the Indo-Mongoloids. S. Endle says that the Kacharis were the original autochthons of the Assam Valley.[23] The *Dimasas* were also called the Kacharis although they themselves prefer to be called as *Dimasa,* and there is some controversy about the origin of the names Cachar (Kachar) and Kachari. S.K. Bhuyan suggested that "the superficial observation is led to suppose that the habitat of the Kachari is Cachar and that it is only in Cachar that the Kacharis experimented the ardous task of state building".[24] According to local traditions and literature of Surma Valley the valley of Barak was known to the people of Sylhet as Kachar and its inhabitants as Kacharis since early times.[25] The word *Dimasa* in their own language means 'sons of the great river'[26] and there is no meaning for Kachar, whereas in Bengali spoken in Surma Valley (Cachar-Sylhet), the deep bank of a river or a tract of land between a river and a hill is designated as Kachari. Gait believed that, "Kachar is derived from a Sanskrit word meaning a 'broadening region'. The district of Cachar may have got its name directly from this word".[27] *Viswakosa* informs that there was in ancient time a village called Kachhal and Cachar got its name from that village.[28] The traditions are still current among the indigenous Bengalee of Cachar about the Kachhal Village. On the other hand, there is no record to suggest that *Dimasa* or any section of the Bodo of Assam were at any time known as Kachari before they ruled in Cachar. As Gait writes, "They were known to the *Ahoms* as Timisa, clearly a corruption of *Dimasa,* so that this name must have been in use when they were still in the Dhansiri valley".[29] The indigenous Bangalees of Cachar,

---

23. *S. Endle; The Kachari,* London, 1911, p. 7.
24. S.K. Bhuyan; (Ed.) *Kachari Buranji* (hereafter KB), Gauhati, 1936, p. XV-VI.
25. P.N. Bhattacharjee; *A Critical Account of Mr. Gait's History of Assam, Allahabad,* 1906,p. 14; A.C. Chaudhury, *Shrihatter Itibritta,* Sylhet, 1317, BS. p. 96.
26. E. Gait; *A History of Assam,* 3rd edtion, Gauhati, 1963, p. 299.
27. *Ibid.,* p. 298.
28. U.C. Guha; *Cacharer Itibritta,* Dacca, 1911, p. 48.
29. Gait; *Op. Cit.* p. 299.

on the contrary, are called as Cacharis as their counterpart in Sylhet are known as Sylhotis. We shall, therefore, for our purpose of this paper use the name *Dimasa.*

State Formation: Early Phase

The *Dimasa* are said to be among the earliest inhabitants of the Assam valley, and they ruled over different states under different names in different times in different parts of that valley.[30] The legends are still current among the *Dimasas* about their *rajya* and *raja* in ancient Kamarupa (Kamruli) and how during a political turmoil they had to cross the big river (Brahmaputra) and a large section of their people were washed away by the river.[31] The Assamese sources give some details about their kingdom at Sadiya and this was probably the first attempt to the Kacharis to built up as independent state after their expulsion from Kamrup".[32] In the neighbourhood of Sadiya was the copper temple of *Kachai Kati,* the tutelar deity of the *Dimasa* and their cognate tribes, which the *Dimasa* rulers continued to worship even after the establishment of their rule in Cachar.[33] There after they shifted to Dimapur (*Dimasapur*) now in Nagaland, in all probability due to the conflicts with Arimatta and his son, Jangle Balahu, the legendary prince of Upper Assam. In the 13th Century, A.D. when the *Ahoms* registered their advent in the Assam valley, the *Dimasa* kingdom extended along the south bank of the Brahmaputra, from Kikhous to Kallang and also included the Dansiri valley and the North Cachar Hills (when South Cachar or the Barak Valley formed part of Tripura).[34] The ramnant of the *Dimasa* palace, forts and tanks still to be found in Dimapur, are suggestive of the process and resources

30. R.M. Nath; *The Background of Assamese Culture,* Shillong, 1949, p.72.
31. Guha; pp. 61-3.
32. *KB*; p. XX.
33. P.N. Bhattacharjee; (Ed.) *Heramba Rajyer Dandavidhi* (hereafter *Dandavidhi*), Gauhati, 1921, p. 11.
34. Guha; p. 66, J.B. Bhattacharjee, "Chronology of the *Dimasa* Rajas of Cachar", *Journal of the North East India Council for Social Science Research,* Vol. II, No. II, Shillong, October, 1978, p.4.

of the state. About the ruins at Dimapur, Gait writes.[35]

"The ruins of Dimapur, which are still in existence, show that, at that period, the Kacharis had attained a state of civilisation considerably in advance of that of the *Ahoms*. The use of brick for building purposes was then practically unknown to *Ahoms*, and all their buildings were of timber or bamboo, with mud-plastered walls. Dimapur, on the other hand was surrounded on three sides by a brick wall of the aggregate length of nearly two miles, while the fourth or southern side was bounded by the Dhansiri river. On the eastern side was a fine brick gateway with a pointed arch and stones pierced to receive the hinges of double heavy doors. It was flanked by octagonal turrets of sold brick, and the intervening distance to the central archway was relieved by false windows of ornamental moulded brick work. The curved battlement of the gateway, as well as the pointed arch over the entrance point distinctly to the Bengali style of Muhammedan architecture. In this connection it will be remembered that, when the *Ahom* King Rudra Singh determined to erect brick buildings at Rangpur, he called in an artisan from Bengal to direct the operations. The excellence of the mortar is shown by the fact that although the building has evidently been shaken on various occasions by earthquakes, it is still in a good state of preservation. Inside the enclosure, (which has not yet been fully explored) are some ruins of temple, or perhaps a market-place the most notable feature of which is a double row of carved pillars of sandstone, averaging about 12 feet in height and 5 feet in circumference. There are also some curious V-shaped pillars which are apparently memorial stones. The nearest point at which the sandstone for these pillars could have been quarried is at least ten miles distant. It seems probable that the blocks of sandstone were brought and set up in the rough and then carved in situ, otherwise they would have been much damnaged in the process of erection. No two are precisely alike in the ornamentation, but all are of one general

35. Gait; p. 302.

form, having large semi-circular tops, with concrete foliated carving below on the shaft. There are representations of the elephant, deer, dog, duck, and peacock head. The inference seems to be that, at this time, the Kacharis were free from all Hindu influences. There are several fine tanks at Dimapur, two of which are nearly 300 yards square".

With the turn of events of the *Dimasas*, however, failed to retain, this fine city for long. The expansionist endeavour of the *Ahoms* envitably clashed with the *Dimasas* and the hostilities between the two are recorded since 1490 A.D. In the first encounter the *Ahoms* were routed and compelled to sue for peace. The rapidly growing power of the *Ahoms*, however, enabled them to exert pressure and, as a result, Khorapna, the *Dimasa* Raja, was pushed to the Dhansiri river. Khunkara, brother of Khorapha, thereupon usurped the authority and renewed the war which continued till his defeat in 1531 A.D. The authority in the *Dimasa* state was then wrested by Dersongpha, son of Khorapha, who entered into agreement with Sulungmung, the Ahom ruler, acknowledging the *Ahom* suzeerainty, but after a few years, he also attempted to regain the ceded territory and was killed in a war with *Ahoms* in 1536 A.D. The *Ahoms* sacked Dimapur, and the *Dimasa* capital was eventually shifted to Maibong in the North Cachar Hills under the leadership of the son of Dersongpha.[36]

Intermediate Phase

The evidence is not enough for an understanding of the process of state formation and state structure of the *Dimasa* either at Sadiya or a Dimapur. But at Maigong the process entered into a crucial phase due to several convenient factors, when they came under the influence of Brahminical Hinduism. The son of Dersongpha, who led the *Dimasas* to Maibong, assumed the name Nirbhoyanarayana and was proclaimed as the Raja.[37] It is interesting to note that all of his

36. S.K. Bhuyan; (ed.), *Deothai Asom Buranji* (hereafter DAB), Gauhati, 1932, pp.4-6; *Assam Buranji* (hereafter *A.B.*), Gauhati, 1930, p.21-2; *K.B.*, pp.14-9; G.C. Baruah, *Ahom Buranji*, Shillong, 1930, pp. 668, Nath, pp. 72-3.
37. Nath; pp. 73; *J.B.* Bhattacharjee; N. 35.

predecessors had tribal names. The tradition[38] suggests that the prince in his difficult time came across a Brahmin, who predicted him good fortune. The prince accepted him as his *Dharmadi Guru (Dharmadhyakshya)* and gave him an important position at the court. The later records suggests that Dharmadi became an important institution in *Dimasa* political system, as he was supposed to advice the Raja on all important matters and interpret the law of the Sastras.[39] The Raja also could discover through the guru that his forefathers had a divine origin, and that their tutelar deity, *Kachai Kati* was only a form of *Sakti*.[40]

The deity quietly transformed into *Ranachandi* (Goddess of War) and the hymn and verses were made available by the Brahmins for her worship. As the *Dimasas* were then locked in prolonged wars with the *Ahoms* and *Jayantia* and had to reckon with the Mughal invasions, the 'Goddess of War' could easily command loyality. Further, the deity was projected as fierce and this corroborated with it original *Kachai Kati* (flesh eaters) form. The success in foiling the repeated *Ahoms* onslaughts strengthened the belief that *Ranachandi* was the protectress for the tribe and worshipping her would ensure victory in the war path. The Brahmins also tried to establish that the *Dimasa* heritage was as old as the *Mahabharata*. It is

---

38. This information was given to the author by Rajkumar Janmajay Barman of Shillong, In his eighties Shir Barman is a retired senior civil servant and belongs to the royal clan of the *Dimasas*.
39. J.B. Bhattacharjee; *"Some Aspects of Heramba Government on the Eve of the British Rule"*, Shohak, Vol. 2, Pt. B. Jaipur 1973, pp. 189-95.
40. A legend also goes that *Ranachandi* appeared in dream to Nirbhoyanarayana and told him to meet her next day at the river side. The raja waited there for a long time and then observed a snake swimming in the river. He believed that the goddess had assumed that form for the interview and took hold of the tail. The snake turned into a sword in his hand, which he carrried to the home. In the same night, *Ranachandi* again appeared to him and told him that he was wrong in not siezing the snake by neck. However, the sword would be the good luck of the state and the state would prosper as long as it was preserved with care. The *Dimasas* having so long" practiced as gloomy demore worship, adopted the rite of *Kali* the wife of the All Destroyer, in her most horrible form and identify her with their own female demon *Ranachandi*". W.W. Hunter; A Statistical Account of Assam, Vol. II, London, 1879, pp. 401-02.

known from *Mahabharata* that when the Pandavas were wandering in the jungles, Bhima the second Pandava married Hidimba, the demons, and Ghatotkach, who later died in the battle of Kurukshetra was born to them.[41] The Brahmins discovered that Hidimba, was the ancestress of the tribe and that Ghatotkach was their first ruler. The Raja also received a genology that began with Bhim-sena and included more than three hundred names (all Sanskrit-Hindu). The Brahmins and important state officials since then maintained the list (called *Hermba-raja-malaya*) and the names of the succeeding rulers were added from time to time. Thomas Fisher, the first Superintendent of Cachar, collected a number of such lists[42] and a few of them are available in print.[43] These lists begin either with Ghatotkachanarayana or with Bhimasena followed by Ghatotkacha and end with Govindachandranayana (died in 1830) but do not confirm with each other either in order or in number. Hunter dismissed them as "Brahminical forgery, invented for the purpose of extolling the importance and pure descent of the dynasty".[44] It can be said about the late rulers that the names were perhaps carried in memory until put down in isolated lists and include the Rajas belonging to dynasties which ruled successively and contemporaneously in different parts of medieval Cachar.[45] There is no doubt that the facts and fictions freely mingled together to give the royal family the dignity of a divine descent. Nevertheless, the list, if at all any, presented to Nirbhoyanarayana by his *Guru* was undoubtedly imaginary. It had, however a strong impact in inspiring the *Dimasa* rulers and aristocracy with intense pride in their Hindu origin and they turned to be the champion of their new faith. The *Dimasa* state also since then came to be called as the *Harmba-rajya* as known from their coins, inscriptions and records.

---

41. The *Mahabharata of Vyasa*, English Translation by P. Lal; Vol. 19, Calcutta, 1970, pp.65-8.
42. *Foreign Political Proceedings* (hereafter FPP) 14 May, 1832, Nos. 100-07.
43. Guha; *Op. Cit.*, pp. 71-4; Hunter; *Op. Cit.*, pp. 403-4; A.C. Choudhury; App. pp. 25-7.
44. Hunter; p. 403.
45. J.B. Bhattacharjee; N. 35.

In line with the situation in Medieval India, the Rajas of Heramba also issued coins like other Hindu Rajas to make their coronation, pilgrimage and victory in wars. The coins contained Hindu legends, in Sanskrit language and Bengali character. A gold coin of Meghnarayana of 1498 *Saka* (1576 A.D.) proclaims him as 'Herabheswara' (ruler of Herambha) and "worshipper of *Ranachandi*".[46] A silver coin of Yasanarayana dated 1505 *Saka* (1583 A.D.) bears the epithet *Hacengsa-Vangsaja* (Hecengsa being one of the *Sengfongs* of clans, and *Hara-Gouri-carana-Kamala.*[47] Pratapnarayana in his coin dated 1528 *Saka* (1606 A.D.) claims himself as the worshipper of *Siva.*[48] So also does Bhamabalanarayana *saka* 1552 (1630 A.D.), Viradarpanarayana, *saka* 1565 (1643 A.D.) and Harischandranarayana, *saka* 1642 (1720 A.D.).[49] Indravallabhanarayana in his coin dated 1560 saka (1638 A.D.) claimed to be worshipper of *Hara-Gouri.*[50]

The earliest inscription was also issued by Meghnarayana in 1498 *saka* (1576 A.D.) on the occasion of the erection of the gateway (*Singha-Dwara*) in Maibong on his accession to the throne.[51] An inscription on a rock-cut temple at Mailbong suggests that it was issued in the *saka* year 1643 (1721 A.D.) by Harischandranarayana and the temple was constructed by him and dedicated to *Ranachandi.*[52] The ruins of Mailbong, it palace complex, the temples and the gateway and the arrangements for its security (watch-houses) that have survived the stress and strain of time and circumstances, in spite of the damages done by major earthquakes recorded since last century and the construction of the railway line

46. *Communication by Vasant Choudhury and Parimal Ray,* 64th session of the Numismatic Society of India (hereafter NSI), Indore, 1976.
47. A.W. Botham; *Catalogue of the Provincial Coin Cabiner, Assam,* Allahabad, 1930, p. 529.
48. Vasant Chowdhury and Parimal Ray, "*Coin-Type of the Kings of Kachar*", *Journal of the Ancient Indian History,* Calcutta University, Vol. *V*, Pt. 1-2, 1971-72, p. 208 (hereafter AIII).
49. *Ibid.* pp. 209-11.
50. *Ibid.* p. 209.
51. Guha; pp. 76-7.
52. For text see A.C. Chaudhury; Pt. II, p. 102.

towards the close of that century, still proclaim the magnificient proportion that the *Dimasa* state had reached during sixteenth to the eighteenth century.

While the Brahminical Hinduism acted as an effective symbol in the process of state formation, another important factor that strengthened the authority of the ruler was confronting relations with the neighbouring states which forced the *Dimasas* to live in a virtual war situation. The Raja had to raise powerful army enlisting almost all the abale bodied males in the state, named the main column as *Chandi Paltan*[53] and in most cases, the heir-apparent to the throne (called *Juwaraj*) served as the commander-in-chief of the army.[54] In their distress, the people looked upon the war goddess as the protectress of the state and this brought them more and more under Brahminical influence. In spite of the fact that the *Dimasas* had abandoned Dimapur, the *Ahoms* maintained pressure from the west to wrest the Kapili-Dayaung-Dhansiri valleys. To strengthen their position, the *Ahom* rulers planted new villages bordering the *Dimasa* state in Nowgong, created new posts of frontier officers and raised cutposts or *chokies* all along the frontier.[55] Nevertheless, despite several encounters the *Dimasas* could maintain their hold in the Nowgong section of the state and maintained forts at vulnerable places.[56] The *Dimasa* Rajas also succeeded in imposing vassalage over the Dimarus state in Kamrup, and clashed for its overlordship with the *Ahoms.*[57]

Meanwhile, the Koches under Chnilaraj subdued the *Ahoms* and forced the Rajas of Dimarua, Khyrim, Jayantia and Manipur to pay tribute. Durlabhanarayana, the *Dimasa* Raja was also defeated in 1562 A.D. and undertook to pay such tribute. The Koches also wrested Cachar Valley from Tripura and subsequently the Koch Governor, Uditnarayana, laid the

---

53. FPP; 14 May, 1832, No., 101.
54. J.B. Bhattacharjee; 35, pp. 4-6.
55. K.B.; pp.xxiii, 44-9.
56. *Ibid.*, pp. 39-45.
57. J.B. Bhattacharjee; *"Jayantia-Heramba Relations", Proceedings of the Indian History Congress,* Muzaffarpur, 1972, pp. 251-4.

foundation of an independent Koch state there with Khaspur as the Capital.[58] During the reverses that the Koches faced during the encounters with the Sultans of Bengal, the *Dimasa* Raja asserted himself as an independent ruler as did his counterparts in Assam, Jayantia etc.[59] On the otherhand, relieved of the Koch dominations, the *Ahom* ruler renewed pressure on the *Dimasa* which Meghnarayana (1576-83 A.D.) had successfully resisted. Jasanarayana (1583-1613 A.D.), the son and successor of Meghnarayana was the most powerful ruler of the *Dimasa* during whose reign the territorial limit of the state expanded considerably. He defeated Dhanamanik, the Raja of Jayantia, in 1576 A.D. and assumed the name Satrudaman, while after defeating Jasamanik the next Raja of Jayantia for sometime became a vassal of the *Dimasa* state. He also defeated Pratap Singha, the *Ahom* monarch, in 1606 A.D. assumed the name Pratapanarayana and changed the name of his capital Maibong to Kirtipur.[60] He also annexed a portion of the Cachar Valley bordering his state and pushed the boundary in the Mughal district of Sylhet. Thereupon he assumed the name Indrapratapnarayana, established two forts in portion of the state annexed from Sylhet at Pratapgarh and Asuritikar[61] (both in modern Karimganj district) and issued a coin in 1524 *saka* (1602 A.D.) wherein he claimed himself as *Shrihattavijayina* or conqueror of Sylhet.[62]

In spite of the initial set back he succeeded in repulsing the Mughal invasion in 1612 A.D.[63] Satrudaman is said to be the hero of a Bengali novel *Ranachandi*, written in Cachar, wherein his heroic role in defeating the Muslims have been

---

58. N.C. Sarma (ed.); *Darangraj Vansavali* (hereafter DRV), Gauhati, 1974, p. 77; Guha, pp. 32-3; J.B. Bhattacharjee, *"The Koch Principalli is Cachar: A study of Medieval Polity Formation in North East India", Proceedings of the North East India History Association*, Second Session, 1981, pp.104-123.
59. J.B. Bhattaharjee; N. 14, p. 4.
60. S.K. Bhuyan; (ed.) *Jayantia Buranji* (hereafter J.B.), Guahati, 1936, pp. 13-6; M.I. Borah (trans.) *Baharistan-i-Ghaiby*, Guahati, 1936, Vol, p. 172.
61. Borah; pp. 21-4, Vol. II, p. 690.
62. A.N. Lahiri;*"A Comprehensive Account of the noteworthy Features of the Hindu coins of North East India"*, NSI, 65th session, Shillong, 1977.
63. Borah; *Op.Cit.*, Vol. II, p. 828.

mentioned.[64] On occasions, however, the Raja of Cachar undertook to pay tribute to the Mughal authority in Bengal[65], but there is no record to suggest that the Mughals ever insisted on the vassalage of Cachar and maxim of the Mughal policy to cultivate friendly relations with the rulers on their distant frontiers.[66]

The *Ahoms* in the seventeenth century were engaged in hostilities with the Mughals and, as a result, they avoided any confrontation with Cachar, Jayadhraj Singha, the *Ahom* ruler even sent some presents to Biradarpanarayana (1643-81 A.D.) and sought military help against Mir Jumalah's invasion.[67] The *Ahom* rulers, however, insisted on tribute from Cachar whenever there was no possibility from Mughal attack. Rudra Singha had forced Cachar and Jayantia to pay tributes to the *Ahoms*, but in his scheme of a northeast confederacy to attack the Mughals in Bengal, Cachar and Jayantia among others were partners and contributed soldiers in the confederated army.[68] The Rajas of Cachar did not pay the tribute for long. The diplomatic correspondences between *Ahoms* and the *Dimasa* court in the later years show that whenever a Raja ascended the *Dimasa* throne the *Ahom* envoys visited him to demand tribute, whereas the ascending ruler demanded bride from the *Ahom* monarch.[69] There are evidences to suggest that the animosity and frontier clashes between the *Ahoms* and the *Dimasas* continued till both the states were superseded by the British in the nineteenth century. Krishna Chandranarayana (1773-1813 A.D.) actively patronised the Moamaria rebels in the *Ahom* state which proved to be an important cause for the fall of the *Ahoms*.[70]

The *Dimasa* rulers of Maibong also succeeded in subduing a large number of Miku and Angami Naga villages. About the

---

64. Gait; p.305.
65. A.C. Roy; *History of Bengal*, Calcutta, 1968, p. 303.
66. J.B. Bhattacharjee; The *Garos and the English*, New Delhi, 1978, p. 19.
67. K.B.; pp. 46-50.
68. *Ibid.*, pp. 98-113.
69. *Ibid.*, pp. 51-58, DAB; pp. 25- 6; *A.B.*, p. 22.
70. S.K. Bhyan; (Trans.) *Tungkhungia Buranji*, Gauhati, 1933, pp. 122-6.

early Angami-*Dimasa* relations, Hutton refers to an interesting legend. This suggests that "When Bhim Raja (Bhimadarpa-narayana, 1615-38) built his great *Kheddαy* at Sonapur. He fell in love with a *Nagini* whom he found in the jungle and became the ancestress of the Diger Kacharis, who pride themselves on their descent".[71]

Another important factor that had contributed to the process of state formation was the possibility of surplus extraction by the state. The *Dimasas* took to plough cultivation in flat and valley lands long back, although the hills they continued with the primitive method of *Jhumming*. In North Cachar Hills, even these days they are both shifting and terrace cultivators.[72] The Central Cachar division was fertile for agriculture and the portion of Nowgong district even now is considered as the granary of Assam. *Gopichander Panchali*[73], a Bengali chronicle written in Cachar in 1670 *Saka* (1748 A.D.), describes the peasants of Davaka as the Children of *Lakshmi* (Hindu goddess of Wealth). The area was directly connected with North Cachar, Manipur, Naga Hills, Assam and Jayantia, and through Kapili route with Sylhet and Cachar valley, and a considerable amount of trade passed through it. Jenkins and Pemberton, who visited this area in the early years of the nineteenth century, noticed the big market in Mohung-Dijua which was visited by large number of traders, from out side, and were highly impressed by the economic prosperity of the tract.[74] No wonder, the Brahmins discovered that the river Kapili that passed through the tract was as Holy as the Ganges. The river came to be recognised as Kapili-Ganga and a holy dip there was part of the annual rituals of the members of the royal family.[75] The annexation of a portion of the Surma Valley in the seventeenth century added to the prosperity of the state and to its revenue. On the authority of *Tripura Buranji*

71. J.H. Hutton ; The *Angami Nagas*, London, 1921, p. 13.
72. Dipali G. Danda; *Among the Domasas of Assam*, New Delhi, 1978, p. 81.
73. By Krishna Mohan; " *Swarnapur of Cachar*", unpublished, Transcription in collection of the author.
74. FPP; 12 November, 1832, No. 46, Robinson, pp. 312.
75. *Cachar Records*, Assam State Archieves, (hereafter Cr), No. 285, of 1839.

it is known that Rungreng in South Cachar was a flourishing market where the people of Cachar, Manipur and Tripura traded.[76]

The early British records suggest that the North Cachar hills and the adjoining hill areas supplied to Bengal timber, precious wood (including sandal) cane, elephant-tusk, rubber, cotton, silk etc.[77] It is also known from Persian sources that Kajaliban in Central Cachar was famous for elephants and the Rajas exported elephants.[78] The Rajas of Cachar also controlled the external trade and levied duty on the transit stations. They also collected land revenue from the plains portion of the state. The hill people were not totally exempted from taxation from Cachar valley. It was a hergoat, a pair of fowls, a duck and two coconut per holding. This was subsequently raised to 12 annas per *Kulbah.*[79] At the time of Kirtichandra this rate was raised to Rs. 3.[80] *Kalicharan Upakhyan.*[81]

---

76. S.K. Bhuyan; (ed.) *Tripura Buranji*, Guahati, 1936, pp. 52-3.
77. W.K. Firminger; (comp.) *Sylhet District Records*, Vol. I, Shillong, 1913, Nos. 32-43.
78. H. Blochhman; "*Koch Behar, Koch Hajo and Assam in the 16th and 17th Centuries,* according to the *Akbarnama, the Badshahnama, and Fatiya-i-Ibriya*", *Journal of the Asiatic Society of Bengal* (hereafter JASB), Vol. XLi, 1872, p. 94.
79. Guha; p. 109.
80. Hunter; p. 415.
81. An unpublished chronicle by Krishna Mohan of Swarnapur, Cachar, Transcript in Collection of the author.
Shata kulbah mati laila rajai diya dhan
tejarati ak khel haila takhan
bhag kari dila kali karmachari gane
karmakar mukhtar majhi jata chhila sane
ak bhag hat lagi dila kali chhari
ar bhage prasadman bandhi nij bhari
ak kuri paik jage praharar lagi
asvashala hatishala kari bhaga bhagi shrigaltekh nagar haila heramba bikhyata
tin sahashra lok bas karigar sahita
hat bare gam gam panch sahashra dari
mani mukhtar kar lay jane jane kari karmacharir kar nai kalicharan kai
sahashra mudra rajkar mukhtar jugai
ramchandra maharaj tate hai raji
chhay char ule diba karila arji
Gopichander Panchali.

A Bengali chronicle composed during the reign of Ramachandranarayana (1728-35 A.D.), gives us interesting information. This is the account of one Kalicharan who was Brahmin but turned to be a trader and the trade with distant markets brought him fortune. He brought in a few families of porter, carpenter weaver, blacksmith, goldsmith etc. artisans and started a *Karkhana-nagar* (industrial township) at a place called "Khalinagar" on the bank of Barak. The Raja allotted to him several hundred *Kulbah* (*Kulbah* = 4.82 acres) of land and thus set up a large estate. Kalicharan paid rupees one thousand annually to the Raja in terms of revenue, and in return, gained the right to send three representatives to the *UI (assembly)*. His own estate came to be recognised as a *Khel (tejarathi-khel)*.

Another important source of income of the state was the contribution made by the ethnic kindred of the tribe in the Assam Valley. The *Dimasa* Raja was looked upon by those 'scattered Kacharis' as lingering symbol of their racial unity and maintained allegiance to the Raja and paid tribute to him. In the beginning of the nineteenth century every family outside the state contributed from one to five rupees annually which was regularly collected by the agents deputed by the Rajas.[82] The financial position of the state as early as in the sixteenth century can be ascertained from the fact that the 1562 the *Dimasa* Raja agreed to pay an annual tribute of seventy thousand gold *mohars* and sixty elephants to the victorious Koch ruler.[83]

The divine origin gained through the corridor of Brahminical influence, leading the people in the war path and the surplus extracted by the state served as an effective instruments in the process of state formation, while the use of Sanskrit and Bengali languages in official transaction helped the Raja in consolidating his position. The Raja emerged as the head of the state and was helped in his administration by the ministers called *Patra* and *Bhandari*. The head of the council of ministers was called *Barbhandari*. These ministers and other

---

82. K.B.; pp. xvii-xviii.
83. DRV; p. 77, A.C. Choudhary, *Op. Cit.*, p.76.

important state officials were from the *Dimasa* tribe. Each division of the tribe, called *Sengfong* sent a representative to the royal court, called *Mel*. The number of *Sengfongs*, however, increased with the perpetuating of the race. According to tradition, originally there were only five *Sengfongs* and in Dimapur the number increased to seven.[84] In Mailbong, during the reign of one Hariram 5 and in that of Mayuradhvaja 4 more were added. Ultimately, during the reign of Krishnachandra the number of *Sengfong* reached forty.[85] The Bengalees from the plains did not directly nor did the state officers interfere in their affairs. Raja Kirtichandranarayana (1735-45 A.D.), as known from a copper-plate[86] grant, appointed one Maniram Laskar of Barkhola as the *Uzir* for the administration of justice and collection of revenue in the portion of the state in South Cachar.

Nevertheless, the Bengalee influence in the court in Maibong is known from various sources. The *Dharmadi Guru or the Raj Pandit,* who was always a Bangali Brahmin, exerted influence in state politics. He was the chief adviser to the Raja and sole interpreter of the Hindu law. The Raj Durbar was also adorned by a galaxy of Brahmin scholars who translated some *puranas* and portions of the epics in Bengali. There are mentions of some books that were written on the basis of *Shastras,* either in Bengali or in Bengali with parallel Sanskrit as administrative manuals. The *Vivad-darpan, Rindan-vidhi, Kalmi Punthi* are among them.[87] The *Cacharir Niam* written during the reign of Tamradhvajanarayana (1699-1708) was the code for the administration of the Bengalee dominated Cachar plains.[88] Bhubaneswar Bachaspati, a Bhattacharya Brahmin of Sylhet was the court poet of Raja Suradarpanarayana

84. Guha; *Op. Cit.*, p. 108.
85. *Ibid.* p. 109.
86. For Text see A.C. Choudhary, *Op. Cit.*, pp. 102-6.
87. J.B. Bhattacharjee; *"Some Important Sources of the History of Medieval and Modern Cachar," Shodhak,* Vol. 4, *Pt., A,* Jaipur, 1975, pp. 460-72.
88. *Dandavidhi, Kh Punthi.*

(1708-20A.D.) and he rendered *Naradiya Rasamitra* in to Bengali. The *Brama Purana* was also translated in his court. Suradarpa himself composed some *Malsi* songs in Bangali. The tradition suggests that the *Dharmadi guru* recited *Bhagavata* in the court every evening and interpreted to the audience.[89] The rajas patronised the Brahmins and the Bengali literature and granted *Devattvara* and *Brahmattvara* lands for the support of the temples and the Brahmins.[90] They also encouraged settlements of the artisans and craftsmen in Mailbong. Mailbong developed into a glorified township. The names of the areas around the palace like Kumararpara, Kamarpara, Dhamadi Haor, Brahmanbra etc.[91] suggest the demographic pattern and Hindu influence in the erstwhile *Dimasa* capital.

The impact of Sanskritisation was spontaneous on the members of the royal family and the aristocracy. The caste system also could make some influence. An analysis of the functions of the various *sengfong* or clan is a pointer. Of the 40 *senfongs*, 5 were royal clans once supplied the ministers, one ambassador, one store-keeper, one correspondent or writers, one cook, one Gardener, one barber and two artisans or craftsmen. The rest had no specific function or status and this might suggest that they were the commoners. In fact the professional specialisation of the various *sengfongs* was the beginning of social stratification of the *Dimasa* society and the increase in the number of such *sengfong* from 7 to 40. The Rajas came form the *Bodosa, Thaosengsa* and *Hasyungsa* in three different stages of the state formation. With the proliferation, new clans came into existence *viz. Songyabsa* (King's Cooks), *Nyablasa* (fishermen), *Nobidasa* (hunters) Bengyasa (servants, slaves and outcasts), *sergasa* (blacksmiths) etc. Besides the Bengalee Bahmins since Hinduisation, there were eight Dimasa *families* attached to

89. *Amit Kumar Naug: "Prachin Cachare Bangla Basa O Sahitya", Sambhar,* Silchar, 1367 BS, pp. 25-7; Jagannath Deb, *"Heramber Itikatha"*, Azad (Nava Vara Sankya) Silchar, 1370, p. 8.
90. J.B. Bhattacharjee *Op. Cit.*, 89.
91. Guha; *Op Cit.*, p. 76.

the court who sacrificed to a particular diety. The high priest Alu Raja was chief spiritual advisor to the Raja. Besides the traditional dieties like *Alow, Mali* and there was one *Bangla Raja* (King of Bengal).[92] The social stratification thus brought in new clans and dieties. Each *Sengfong* sent a representative each to the *Mel,* but in the *Mel Mandap* (council hall) representatives were offered seats according to the status of the *sengfong* one represents in a hierarchical order.[93] This assembly, however, continued to be a powerful organisation in state politics and it maintained that it had the authority to elect the Raja. When Raja Suradarpanarayan died young and without a son, his mother Rani Chandraprava nominated Kirtichandranarayana of the collateral line to the throne with approval of the *sengfong* and the ministers.[94] The right to such selection or nomination was however, limited to a candidate belonging to the royal clan. The Rajas had matrimonial connection with the Hinduised tibal royal families of Assam, Cooch Behar, Manipur, Jayantia and Tripura.[95] Many of them had more than one wife and number of concubines and in case of matrimonial alliance the brides were accompanied by slaves.[96]

Final Phase

The process of state building in Mailbong that started with Nirboyanarayana reached its climax during the reign of Kirti chandranarayana (1735-45A.D.) who was assisted in state affairs by more than fifty *Patra* or ministers and appointed an *Uzir* for the administration of South Cachar and an *Aditya* for Central Cachar. By the time his son, Gopichandranarayana (1745-57A.D.) became the Raja the state was fairly large and prosperous and by an accident the Koch state in Cachar valley

92. *Ibid.,* C.A. Soppitt, N. 9, pp. 25-48 J.H. Crace;"*The Hill Cacharis*", *Census of India,* 1931, Vol.I, Pt. 8.
93. Guha; p. 104-6.
94. FPP; 14 May, 1832, No. 100.
95. K.B., p.xxiii, J.B., pp. 33-4; Guha pp. 80-1, *Rajamala (Royal Chronicle of Tripura)* Agarthala, 1974, p. 3, *Vihayt Panchali* (Royal Chroncicle of Manipur) Imphal, 1967, pp. 16-9.
96. *Vijay Panchali,* p. 39; K.B., p. 20.

merged with the *Dimasa* state, *Gopichander Panchali,* written during his reign, gives some interesting details of his administration. His coronation *(Abhisekha)* was conducted by eleven Brahmin priests (presumably according to Vedic rites). Flood was, as it is even now an annual feature in Cachar Valley and caused untold sufferings to the poor peasantry. Gopichandra introduced a festival, called Barak Puja for propitiation the mighty river and the *Panchali* claims that since then there was no flood which increased his popularity. He also brought in additional families of Brahmins from Bengal and granted Lands for their settlement. The Raja maintained diplomatic relations with the neighbouring states, and his prowess caused anxiety to his neighbours. He conquered the lands of the *Kukis* and appointed *Raja* and *Mantri* from their own folk. The *Vaisya* community of Cachar then maintained boat-bound trade with Bengal. Among the artisan castes *Kumar, Kamar, Yogi sutradhar* etc. have found mention in the text. It also informs that there were large markets in the borders of the state which were visited by merchants from Burma and China, besides those from Bengal and the *Firingis* (Europeans).

During the reign of Gopichandra, his son Harischandra was the *Juvaraj* and the commander-in-chief of the army, while his nephew Lakshmichandra was the *Aditya* or the head of Dharmapur *visaya* (Central Cachar or Nowgong section).[97]

Meanwhile, Bhim Singha the raja of the Koch state in Cachar grew old and his only daughter, Kanchain was married to Lakshmichandra.[98] As a result, the two states merged together. According to the historian of Cooch Behar this took place in 1745. This was also the year of Gopichandra's accession to the throne, Shortly afterwards, Bhim Singh died and the capital of Cachar was shifted from Maibong to Khaspur (the former seat of the Koch state). Gopichandra was suceeded by his son, Harischandra II

---

97. FPP, 14 May 1832, No. 100.
98. J.B. Bhattacharjee; *"The Koch Principality in Cachar: A Study of Medieval Polity Formation in North East India", Proceedings of the North East History Association,* Second session, 1981, pp. 104-23.

(1747-72A.D.) but he preferred the life of a *Sannyasin* (popularly know as *Baul Raja* and abdicated in favour of his cousin, Lakshmichandranarayana (1772-73A.D.).[99] The latter, however, died only about a year after without leaving any issue. So Krishnachandra (1773-1813A.D.), the minor son of Harischandra, ascended the throne. He too died without any issue, and was succeeded by his brother Govindachandra-narayana (1813-30A.D.) whose reign was the end of the *Dimasa* rule in Cachar. He became unpopular by marrying the widow of his leader brother which was permitted neither by Hindu nor by *Dimasa* custom. The forty *Senfongs* turned hostile towards him and Tularam established himself as the independent ruler of northern and central divisions of the state with British intervention. The fugitive princes of manipur usurped the authority in Cachar and forced Govindachandra to take refuge in British Bengal. This was followed by the Burmese occupation of Cachar and the declaration of war against Burma by the British which resulted in the expulsion of the Burmese and the reinstitution of Govindachandra as the tributary ruler of Cachar, but he was assassinated in 1830A.D. As he had no legal successor, the British annexed Sough Cachar in 1832A.D. The latter also forced Tularam to surrender Central Cachar in 1834, and in 1854 North Cachar was also annexed by them when Tularam was pensioned off.[100]

The final phase of the state formation was experienced in Khaspur and here two methods that worked most was Sanskritisation (Brahminical Hindu) of the royal family and aristocracy and the large scale use and patronisation of Bengali language and literature. With the shifting of the capital to Khaspur, the members of the royal family and aristocracy moved to the Cachar plain. They came to constitute a Hindu caste called *Barman*, proclaimed by the Brahmins as *Kshatriya* and allowed to use sacred thread.[101]

---

99. *Ibid.* pp. 136-8.
100. J.B. Bhattacharjee; N. 1, pp. 124-129.
101. T. Fisher; *"Memoir of Sylhet, Kachar and the Adjacent districts"* JASB, 1840, pp. 13-6.

Some of the Bengalee Brahmins served them as priests,[102] although they were for this looked down upon by the members of their own community.[103]

Along with the Hindu rites they also practiced some of their traditional rites, including sacrifices for the health of the Raja and the safety of the people. As Hunter puts it[104] "These sacrifices were handed down from primitive times, and could only be performed by the descendants of the native Cachari priests. Among them was a human sacrifice from the Raja celebrated on certain occasions."

Harischandra II constructed the palace complex of Khaspur, and the temple of Ranachandi was an added feature. Krishnachandra married in the Vaishnavite royal family of Manipur and under latter's influence embraced *Vaisnavism.* He constructed a *Vishnu Mandir* and a *Snan Mandir* in the capital. The Rajas patronised all forms of Hindu worship *Sakta, saiva* and *Vaisnava* and constructed a large number of temples and tanks in the name of the Hindu dieties. The *Siva* temple in Bhutan hill and *Vishnu* temple in Subang established during the Tripuri rule and the *Kachakanti Kali* in Udharband of the former Koch Rajas were maintained in good condition.[105] They also made large number of land grants for the maintenance of the temples and the brahmins as hereditary *Sebayat* some of which still survive in Cachar Valley. The palaces, called *Pat* were constructed in various parts of the valley for the residential use of the royal family, and those like *Rajar Pat, Ranir Pat, Harischander Pat, Krishnachander Pat, Govindachander Pat* etc. one comes across even today.

Krishnachandra and Govindchandra were staunch *Vaishnava.* Although they had been admitted to Hindu fold they were not given a status in the caste Hindu society and the Brahmins and the other high castes (*Kayastha* particularly)

102. Guha; *Op Cit.*, p. 112.
103. Hunter; *Op. Cit.*, p. 396.
104. *Ibid.*, p. 395.
105. R.M. Nath; *Antiquities of Cachar,* Silchar, 1981, pp. 1-30.

would not take water from them. A metric saying,[106] popular in Cachar says that one day Krishnachandra invited the Majumdar of Bikrampura and asked him to choose between the sword and the glass of water that the Raja had placed on a table. The majumdar took the sword and said that this weapon would help him to protect his caste. The Raja felt insulted and he invited an assembly of the Brahmins to suggest the way of getting a proper place in the Hindu society. As advised by the Brahmins, the Raja performed the *Haranya-garva* ceremony in 1790 A.D. Raja Krishnachandra, his brother Govindachandra and the members of the royal aristocracy entered the body of the gold-plated effigy of the cow and on emergence from it they were proclaimed to have taken rebirth as pure Hindu of the *Khatriya* Caste.[107] On completion of the ceremony the Brahmins divided the gold plate among themselves. They were fed on Rajas cost. In the feast that followed Rajakrishnachandra and Govindachandra served water to the Brahmins.[108] The local traditions suggest that many of the Dimasas got admission to the Caste Hindu society through the corridor of the expensive ceremonies subsequently.[109] It is, however, not known whether they got a genuine *Kshatriya* status in the caste Hindu society. On the contrary, there are evidences that the Brahmins who accepted water from them were charged with degeneration and impurity and called *"Cachari Brahman"* by the late comer Brahmins and the inter-marriage between the two sections of the Brahmins was discouraged.[110]

Along with Brahminical Hinduism the use of Bengali language served as an effective instrument in the process of state building. The *Dimasa* rulers used Bengali in state affairs and patronised Bengali literature since the capital was in

---

106. Guha, *Op. Cit.*,p. 111.
"akjan haite jadi jati raksha pay
prandiya jnanabanta se karje daray"
107. *Hunter, Op.Cit.*,p. 401.
108. Guha, *Op.Cit.*,p. 112.
109. *Ibid.*
110. *Assam Secretariat Records* (hereafter ASR), *Home Misc, B.Progs*, October, 1883, Nos. 136-7.

Maibong, but in Khaspur the use and the patronage became extensive. The members of the royal family and aristocracy and, as matter of fact, all those *Barman* who settled in Cachar Valley had adopted Bengali language. The process of cultural Bengali language. The process of cultural and linguistic assimilation was rather fast in the reigns of the later Rajas. This was important as the Cachar plains was a natural extension of Bengal plains and inhabited by the Bengalees. The land grants, appointment of officials, correspondence, statutes and ordinances, some of which have in the meantime been published[111] were in all Bengali. The Penal Code intoduced by Govindachandra in 1817 was in Bengali with parallel Sanskrit in Bengali character.[112] The last two Rajas of Cachar, Krishnachandra and Govindachandra were known for their contribution to Bengali literature. Krishnachandra's *Ramlilamitra* and *Vasanta-Vihar* are very famous. Govindachandra was proficient in Sanskrit as well. He himself taught Sanskrit to the son of a Brahmin of Kalain and conferred upon him the title of Vidyalankar.[113] The rajas also granted scholarships to the children of the Brahmins and Kayasthas of the state for education in Bengal.[114] They also encouraged the Brahmins in their literary persuits. Some of the well known *Dimasa* scholars, *e.g.* Maniram Barman, Anantaram Barman and Chandra Mohan Barman also contributed to Bengali literature. The manuscripts in the collection of the Normal School Library, Silchar and elsewhere speak a volume about the standard of literary culture during that period.[115]

The extensive rituals, the patronage to temples, Brahmins and educations, maintaining the large royal households and running the administration involved expenditure which the Rajas has to meet out of the collections. The sources of income

111. Guha, *Op. Cit.*, pp. 174-7; A.C. Choudhury; *Op.Cit.*, pp. 104-9; P.N. Bhattacharjee, N. 13.
112. A.C. Choudhury; pp. 108-9.
113. Guha; p. 130.
114. D. Datta (ed.) *Cachar District Records*, Silchar, 1969, p. 12.
115. *J.B. Bhattacharjee, "Hermamba Raj Darbare Bangla Bhasa O Sahitya"Jatak*, Vol.I, Shillong, 1977, pp. 1-6

included land revenue, taxation, of the mines and minerals, the control exercised by the state on export and import[116] and the duty levied on the transit stations and the markets and collections on festive occasions.[117] The Rajas encouraged fresh immigration from Bengal and settlement of the peasant castes[118] for reclaiming the fallow lands. It is possible that while the immigration of the Brahmins and the high castes was encouraged to enhance the status of the state and to man its administration, such encouragement to the peasants was for the purpose of multiplying the revenue. For the payments of the land revenue the members of a *khel* were individually and collectively responsible. How desperate the Rajas were to bring the land under tillage can be illustrated by the fact that in case a peasant had failed to cultivate any portion of his holding action was taken against such defaulters which involved fine and confinement.[119] At the time of Raja Krishnachandra land revenue was at the rate of 12 *Kahan* per *Kulbah* (1 rupee-5 *khan*).[120] Govindachandra raised it to Rs. 6/-. The Rajas collected duty on forests, ferries and fisheries, cattle trade, salt, wells, transit etc. There was also a special tax, called *bandhan* which meant that during *Durga Puja* and other festivals the heads of the villages or agricultural guilds were required to supply certain commodities to the palaces as demanded by the Raja and as per the quota fixed or the area on fixed dates. These items included rice, milk, goat, fowl, etc. The demands sometimes proved exhorbitant on the masses, particularly because the headmen always wanted to retain a portion for them. Those unable to contribute were subjected even to physical torture, to avoid which many of them fled to the jungles.[121] Such torture was reported more during the reign of Krishnachandra who

116. *Revenue Report of Cachar*, 1853; W.J. Allen, *Report on the Administration of District of Cachar*, Calcutta, 1859.
117. *India Political Despatch to the Court of Directors*, No. 25 of 1830.
118. Fisher; *Op. Cit.*
119. Hunter; p. 399.
120. Guha; p. 123; Hunter; p. 415.
121. *Ibid.*

undertook a number of expensive pilgrimages and had to maintain a large household which included his 13 wives.[122]

According to a modest estimate the revenue at the time of Krishnachandra amounted to Rs. 1,00,000 annually.[123] A very important portion of the revenue came from trade and transit duty. The state's trade with Bengal was extensive and in the matter of collection, the Rajas had dispute with the collectors of Sylhet in the early days of the East India Company in Bengal and Krishnachandra had to complain to the Governor-General.[124] Manipur's trade with Bengal also passed through Cachar, and the Rajas used to levy toll at Jirighat where the merchandise form Manipur entered Cachar.[125] For the goods entering Bengal, the levying station was Seallekh which was an important port on Barak in Cachar-Sylhet border.[126]

According to a tradition a former Raja of Cachar had artificially opened a river channel called *Kalakhal* which connected Dhalewari river with Barak at Sealtekh.[127] Besides providing line of water communication for the boats for trade purposes this canal was also used for irrigation for agriculture. The state maintained the monopoly for trade in elephant tusk and ivory.[128] Govindachandra obtained the virtual monopoly of the entire volume of frontier trade as the state suffered loss of revenue due to internal rebellions[129] and the Manipuri and Burmese invasions when a large section of the peasantry was forced to migrate to Bengal.[130] The Raja had to exlpore other means of revenue as well. One of these was the sale of the titles like *Choudhury. Majumdar, Laskar, Bhuiya* etc. on money payment to the Raja and the rates varied

122. *Ibid.*, p. 114.
123. R.B. Pemberton; *Report on the North East Frontier of British India*, Calcutta, 1835, p. 196.
124. S.N. Sen (Comp.) *Prachin Bangala Patra Sankalan*, Calcutta, 1942, Letter No. 65.
125. CR; No. 35 of 1837; FPP, 30 May 1829, Nos. 2-5.
126. *Ibid.*, No. 78 of 1844.
127. Hunter; p. 366.
128. FPP, 9 April, 1829, No. 44.'
129. *Ibid.*, 12 January, 1824, No. 6.
130. Pemberton; p. 196-7.

from Rs. 100/- to 25/-[131] in his code introduced to his treasury.[132] The taxation was indeed, exhorbitant since 1826 when Govindachandra was reinstated as the ruler of a protected state and was required to pay a tribute of Rs. 10,000/- annually to the East India Company.[133]

The financial difficulties were also caused by the fact that the northern and central divisions of the state ceded since 1829[134] under Tulaman Senapati and the Raja was deprived of the income from those areas.[135] Otherwise, the state expanded when the Koch state merged with it. Gopichandra subjugated some Kuki areas and organised it unto several divisions (*khanda*) each or which gave the Raja one elephant annually as tribute.[136] The Rajas also exercised suzerainity over the Kacha Naga areas of Manipur through which considerable trade occurred[137] and Krishnachandra even annexed a portion of the *Angami Naga* territory.[138]

Decline

Krishnachandra and Govindachandra gained unpopu-larity on many counts. The *Dimasa* rulers and the aristocracy became the champions of their new faith and were particular about rites and ceremonies. The Rajas performed expensive religious ceremonies. In the early days of the East India Company's rule they visited religious shrines like Navadwpa, Banaras and Hardwar.[139] For his pilgrimage in 1786,

131. Guha; p. 131.
132. Dandavidhi, K. Punthi.
133. *FPP*, 3 July, 1827, Nos. 42.
134. *Ibid.*, 14 August, 1829, Nos. 5-7.
135. *Ibid.*, 30 May, 1829, Nos. 2-5; 14 May, 1832, No. 83A.
"kukiparbat jay kari karil bistar
khanda khanda kari tar karila sanskar
raja mantri patidila ichchha khushi tar
khanda prati ak hati kar patribar"
Gopichandrer Panchali
136. *FPP*, 30 May 1829, No.1.
137. *A Machenzie; History of the Relations of the Government with the Hill Tribes on the North East Frontier of Bengal*, Catcutta, 1884, p. 345.
138. Sen; Nos. 100, 106-8.
139. Sen; Nos. 100, 106-8.

Krishnachandra raised Rs. 80.000/- by additional taxation.[140]

He also borrowed money from the Governor General with whom he had an audience in Calcutta.[141] A record pertaining to the reign of Govindachandra shows that the state made budgetary provision for expenses in connection with various Hindu festivals throughout the bengali calender.[142] These before long proved to be injurious for the state. These Rajas could not attend to the state matters with essential regularity and the unscrupulous nobles took advantage of the situation.[143] The reaction of the *Dimasa* in the hills was pretty sharp. The *Sengfongs* complained about the violation of the customary laws and usages by Govindachandra, and Tularam took up the leadership of the discontented tribals in the hills.[144]

The transformation of the tutelary diety to *Ranachandi* was not much felt by the *Dimasas*. But more and more adherence to the Brahminical Hinduism and priestly order, and indeed a competition for it, in not too distant a future clashed with their own institutions. Those in the hills, known as *Den* or *Parbatia* were culturally less affected by the change as they continued to practice their tribal rites inspite of the increasing influence of Hinduism on them as well.[145]

The conservative reaction to royal patronage to Brahminism was noticed even earlier. Harischandranarayana I (1730-38A.D.), who in his coronation coin described himself as the worshipper of *Siva*[146] issued an inscription next year to profess his devotion of *Ranachandi* (*Sri-Sri- Ranachandi-pudharvnd-madhukarasya*).[147] Lakshmichandranarayana (1772-73 A.D.) who had constructed a number of temples, claimed

140. Guha; p. 117.
141. For text see Guha; p. 181-2.
142. Sen, Nos. 106, 112-4, 124.
143. FPP, 14 May, 1832, No. 82.
144. *Ibid.*
145. Vasant Choudhury and Parimal Ray; *"A Unique Gold Coin-Type of the Kachari Kings", Monthly Bulletin of the Asiatic Society,* Vol. V. No. 9, pp. 4-5.
146. A.C. Choudhury; p. 102.
147. AIH, p. 211.

himself in his coin as "A bee in the honey of the lotus feet of *Ranachandi*".[148] Even Govindachandra, in a coin, professed his devotion to *Ranachandi*.[149] This coin was struck in 1736 Saka (1814 A.D.) when the Raja was already faced with problems with the *Sengfong* for marrying Induprova, the widow of his elder brother, which the *Sengfong* declared as untenable in their system of *Gandabuh Biah* (*Gandharva-Vivaha*).[150] These might be some of the attempts desperately resorted to by the Rajas to pacify the tribal subjects. As the latter events proved it, they failed to contain the growing dissensions and consequent social tension.

The reaction of the Muslim subjects was also considerable and, under the leadership of a *fakir* a section of them took up arms and forced the Raja to retire to the jungles for sometime.[151] The songs composed by Krishnachandra and Govindachandra during their exile and addressed to *Ranachandi* are still current in Cachar.[152] The series of statues introduced by Govindachandra [153] which prescribed physical torture and fine for crimes against the Brahmins and the high castes committed by the members of these castes provoked rataliation on the part of the lower castes. These facts coupled with British expansionism, hastened the fall of the *Dimasa* state.

State Structure

The most developed phase in *Dimasa* state was a monarchy of the Indian pattern at the head of which was the Raja as supreme authority. He had a divine origin and destined to rule over the people as the 'right hand' of the God. This concept was carefully projected in all documents of the state whether in copper-plate, in stone and rock inscriptions,

---

148. *Ibid.*, p. 208.
149. FPP, 9 April, 1829, No. 44.
150. Sen; No. 77; FPP, 14 November, 1823, No. 19.
151. Guha; p. 113-4.
152. A.C. Choudhury; pp. 25-7.
153. For Texts see K.B., p. 62; Guha; pp. 174-8; A.C. Choudhury; pp. 25-7.

or in *Bhutia* paper. The Hindu symbol and legends were used in such documents where the Rajas claimed themselves as *Harambeswara or Harambadhiswara*. Several Sri (sometimes 108) were used before the name of the Raja and suffixed by *Maharajadhraja, Rajendra, Nripakulacudamani* etc. They were also projected as all powerful (*pracandapratapa*).[154]

The functional authority in the state was vested in the *Patra* and *Bhandari*. The *Barbhandari* held the position of the prime minister. The ministers were drawn from the tribal and the Bengali subjects. The *'Raj Darbar'* (royal assembly) consisted of two wings *mel and ul* meant for the subjects in the hills and the plains respectively where the representatives of the people decided important issues. Only on matters of common interest like deciding measures during foreign invasions the two houses had common sittings. The *Raj Pandit* (a Bengalee Brahmin) was the chief interpreter of Hindu law, and *Qazi* (a Bengalee Muslim) was the expert of the law of Quran. The Raj Pandit, however, had a permanent position in the court. He was the chief councellor to the Raja and perhaps, in the court hierarchy he enjoyed the position next to the Raja. For the administration of north Cachar Hills the Raja appointed a Governor called *Senapathi* who was assisted by a *Bhandari* and both of these officials could be appointed only from the *Dimasa* tribe. The head of the local administration in Central Cachar was called *Aditya* (sometimes *serwal*). To these important positions, including that of the commander-in-chief of the army, the *Juvaraj* (heir apparent) and other members of the royal family were generally appointed. However, during the reign of Govindachandra one Krishnaram Aditya a Bengalee, was the *Serwal* of Dharampur.[155] Govindachandra also once appointed Gambhir Singh as the commander-in-chief[156] (which proved dangerous for his authority as Gambhir Singh and his brothers usurped the authority and forced the Raja to take refuge in Bengal).

154. FPP, 14 May 1832, No. 83A.
155. *Ibid.*, 14 November, 1923, No. 19.
156. Guha; p. 161.

The actual administration of the state was, however, run through autonomous local organisations, both in the hills and the plains. In the hills, the *Dimasas* maintained their tribal institutions. The tribe was divided into 40 sub-tribes of clans, called *sengfong*, and the heads of these forty *sengfongs* sometimes collectively decided important matters. The representatives of the *sengfongs* and *Dimasa* ministers constituted the *Mel*. An appeal, could, of course, be made to the Raja for the decisions, but the latter actually did not interfere in tribal affairs, particularly when because of the profession of Hindu faith he moved away from the *Dimasa* way of life. As a result *sengfongs* enjoyed full authority in local affairs and the *senapati* of the hills looked after the general administration and the *bhandari* collected the revenue. Govindachandra had created three divisions in the Kapili-Dhansiri-Dayung valleys in the northern and central Cachar, *viz*. Dharmpur, Dsvaka and Alanka or asalu each under *serwal*.[157] Earlier Lakshmichandra had conferred upon the important persons in North Cachar hills the title of *Baruah*[158] perhaps in line with the *Ahom* state.

The Raja also did not interfere in the affairs of the Bangalee subjects in the Cachar plains where *khel* system an institution peculiar in Cachar-prevailed as an instrument of local administration. The system developed under peculiar situation. The Barak valley in the remote past was thinly populated due to its unhealthy climate, ravages of the river and the raids of the hill tribes from the neighbourhood. When the population pressure on the adjoining areas of Bengal mounted up the peasants castes extended their settlements in that valley. The original setters came in batches and reclaimed fallow lands. The area brought under use by them in goups came to be known as *Raj* and its ownership was collectively vested in the members. They used to select a headman, called

157. *Ibid.*, p. 98.
158. J.B. Bhattacharjee," *Colonialism and Feudalism*: Cachar in the Nineteenth Century," *Proceedings of the Indian History Congress*, Hyderabad, 1978, pp. 832-5.

Muktar. When the valley passed under the *Dimasa* rulers of Maigong, the Raja did not interfere in its administration and made the *muktar* responsible for the payment of revenue and the civil and judicial administration. The Raja also encouraged immigration from Bengal in groups and allowed them to settle and bring fallow lands under tillage. In the process ten such Raj came up and the Cachar Valley in even today known as *Dash-raj*. As the immigration continued the late-comers were asked to join in either of the *Raj*. When the *Raj* grew in size and population, each of them was divided into smaller units, called *Khel*.[159]

In the early British records these *khels* have been variously described as agricultural guild, corporation or commonwealth[160], as the voluntary association was primarily for agriculture. A *khel* could also be set up for mining (salt well) and fishing and elephant catching but they had to be affiliated to the *Raj* in which one was located, Each *Khel* had a *Mukhtar*, each *Raj* a *Raj-mukhtar*. Ultimately, the *mukhtars* of all the *Raj* constituted a league or union (*Dash-Raj*), of which the *Raj-Mukhtar* of Bikrampur was the head as that was the oldest *Raj* in Cachar. Originally the *Mukhtar* of a *Khel* was elected by the members within it, and the *Raj Mukhtar* by the constituent *Khel-Mukhtar* in all cases to be confirmed by the raja who also reserved the right to dismiss an incompetent, disloyal or corrupt incumbent. In course of time, however, the institution became hereditary and the *Muktars* came to be known as *Laskar* or *Bhuiyas*. The *laskars* and the *Bhuiyas* were later on graded as *Barbuiya, Majer Bhuiya, chota Bhuiya and Barlaskar, Majer laskar, Chota Lasker,* according to the size revenue and importance of the *Khel*. The titles in all cases subsequently passed of as hereditary for the concerned families. Raja Krishnachandra during one of his pilgrimages enjoyed the hospitality of a Raja in Bengal and found that the important people there had such titles as Choudhury, majumdar etc. On

159. *Ibid*.
160. FPP, 3 September, 1830, No. 38, ASR, file No. 636 of 1872, *Cr*, No.62 of 1836; B.C. Allen; *Assam District Gazetteers*, Vol. I. (Cachar), Allahabad, 1906, p. 30.

his return he decided to confer such titles upon the important persons in his own state as this would enhance its prestige. As he died shortly afterwards, Govindachandra could implement the decision. He, however, conferred the titles only in return of money payment. A number of the well-to-do people obtained the titles of Choudhury, Majumdar, Bhuiya and Laskar for themselves and their descendants by paying Rs.100/-, 75/-, 50/- and 25/- respectively.[161]

A *Mukhtar* in any case was an important official of the state. He was the collector of revenue and the civil and criminal judge. The obligation of the *Khel* towards the state "constituted in, firstly, the payment of the revenue, and secondly, the discharge of certain customary services. The latter included the supply of labour for the Rajas works, and of necessaries to him on his progress".[162]

The revenue to be paid by an individual family was decided on the basis of the area of land under its use and tillage, but the revenue of the *Khel* was fixed on the Mukhtar. A shorter of the khel was responsible not only to pay his own share of revenue but also collectively for others. In case an individual sharer became a defaulter, others were required to make good the arear. So also, the *khels,* were individually and collectively responsible for the total share of revenue of the Raj. Theoretically, the state fixed the revenue to be paid by the *Raj;* the *Raj-mukhtar* for the constituent *khels,* and the *Khel-mukhtar* for its sharers. The *khel-mukhtar* deposited his collection with the *Raj-mukhtar,* retaining of course a portion of it towards his commission, and the *Raj-mukhtar* acted as the magistrate in respect of the *khel* and had the authority to order corporal punishment and fine. The death sentence could be passed by the Raja only. In case of dispute between the members belonging to two or more *khels,* the *Raj-mukhtar* was the appropriate authority and while the parties belonged to different *Raj,* the *raj-mukhtar* of Bikrampur would seat over the judgement with the help of his counterparts from the

161. Guha; p. 131.
162. Hunter; p. 396.

concerned raj. In all cases an appeal could be made to the *Raja* who disposed of the matter with the help of the *Raj pandit* in case of Hindu subjects and the *Qazi* in case of the Muslim subjects. As Hunter write.[163]

"The King retained his judicial prerogative in all heinous offences, such as murder and there seems to be some probability that the *bara bandhari* (cachari chief law-man) the *raj pandit* (Hindu spiritual guide to the king), and the *bara mazumdar* (principal union representative) acted as a sort of Judicial committee to advise the Raja in capital cases where a Bengali was concerned. The fact that the Hindu civil code depended upon the *sastras* and the Musalman code on the *Kuran* of both of which the Cachari Raja was equally ignorant, forced the immigrants to depend on some voluntary organisation for settling their internal disputes, and their headmen were thus entrusted with certain fiscal and criminal powers. These criminal powers depended upon the representative status of the league-heads, and not upon the title conferred by the Raja. Thus, the chief criminal power was vested not in a *choudhury,* but in the *mazumdar* or Bikrampur, who became *Bara mazumdar,* and as such above all the *chaudhuris* in the state. While the fiscal and criminal administration was thus provided for with the minimum of royal interference, civil disputes were settled without any interference whatever. In case of a difference between the sharers of *Khel,* the matter was referred to the *khel-mukhtar,* who probably took the advices of the elders on the subject if he could not settle the dispute, the question was referred to the Raj-mukhtar or union representative. In disputes between khels, the court of the first instance was the league Head, who, with the assistance of a council selected from the different *khels* within his *Raj,* heard and decided the case. It is not clear whether any legal organisation existed for enforcing such decrees, but the fiscal and criminal powers of the *Raj-mukhtar* gave him a large and loose authority, and as a matter of fact, his decree was enforced by the imprisonment of any person

163. *Ibid.,* pp. 398-9.1

who delayed to obey. In difficult or keenly contested cases, an appeal or reference could be made to the Raja. In such cases, the sovereign consulted the *Raj pandit* if the parties were Hindus and that officer repeated the *sastras* and laid down the law. In musalman cases the raja consulted with whoever was the chief acknowledged exponent, for the time being, of the Kuran, stories are still current now, when a Hindu case came up, the Raja asked his *pandit* what the sacred texts said. The pandit declared them. The Raja answered, 'It is just' and made due obeisance to the pandit, gave him a present, and decided the case."

An interesting aspect of these *khels* was the secular attitude in voluntary association. As Hunter observed, "by the development of this system, the Bengalis practically obtained a constitution, which in quiet times was sufficient to preserve them from all interference on the part of the royal officers".[164] About the nature of the associations he said.[165] Just as in Hindu communities the village forms the basis of the agricultural commonwealth, which is bound together, theoretically or practically, by ties of kindred and caste, so the *khel* formed the unit of the agricultural community of Cachar, but it members were not connected by any ties of kindred, caste, nationality, or creed. From the first Musalmans and Hindus are found side by side in the same *Khel*; and now that this principle of voluntary association has been extended to other enterprises, no bar of race or creed in opposed to the admission of any part of the population. Thus there are instance of association for leasing fisheries or catching elephants, which include not only Bengali of every caste and creed, but *Kukis, Nagas,* and even Europeans.

The land outside these *khels* was considered *khas* or that belonged to the Raja. These included also the *Debottvara* and *Brahmottvara* grants. There were some *debottvara khels* the income of which were appropriated to meet the expenditure

164. *Ibid.*, p. 396.
165. *Ibid.*, p. 395.

of the important temples, *viz.* income of *paikan* towards *Ranachandi,* Visnugarh towards Lakshminarayana, Vising towards Shyama Kali etc. there were also some *Lakhirajakhels* for the maintenance of the members of the royal family and the ministers. For example, *Khelna* for the Raja, *Mahadevi* for the queen, *Deka Turai for* the heir apparent, *sang Jurai* for the princess, *Patrawala* for the ministers etc.[166] Even in these days one comes across areas like *Rajarmar-Khel.*

In addition to the members of the court and the heads of *khel* and *Sengfong* the state had very few officials. The *Chandy Paltan* was the regular wing of the army under as Senapati. The main body of the soldiers, however, came as the contribution of Raj as per quota fixed from time to time[167]. They also maintained forts along the frontiers at strategic points. It is, however, evident that during the record period of history of the state, the army organisation was never satisfactory. The weaknesses became crystal clear when the state had to face the rebellion of Tularam and the Burmese and the Manipuri invasions. Krishnachandra and Govindachandra had to ask the British government from time to time to help with certain number of soldiers.[168] The Raja maintained a regular palace guard, so also for the members of the royal family and the ministers.[169] There are mentions of *paik* and *prahari* in the chronicles[170] and in local usage they are current till today. The policing was done through the *dakuahs* who were employed by them, besides police, in revenue and miscellaneous duties. The word *Dakuah* possibly indicated that they were originally employed as messengers.[171]

Each *Khel* sent its representative to the *ul.* The number of representative *per khel* was decided on the basis of its size, and the terms of representation was one year during which the

166. FPP ; 3 September, 1830, No.38; Guha; p. 122.
167. Guha; p. 134.
168. FPP; 14 November, 1823, No. 19.
169. *Ibid.,* 14 May, 1830, No. 38.
170. Gopichanderer Panchali.
71. B.C. Allen; *Op. Cit.,*p. 143.

representatives were supposed to stay in the capital.[172] The presence of these representatives and the Brahmins in the capital increased the influence of the Bengalees in court, the important offices including those of the *Vakil* (*agent/ ambassador*) were held by the Bengalees.[173] The offices meant for the plains were filled up by them only, and those who held official position in the long run constituted the privileged class with royal blessings. In addition to the *Mukhtars*, there were other offices which too became hereditary in nature. The *Mukhtars* commanded social responsibility and wealth as well. Besides being the principal sharer in each *khel* they were entitled to a share of collection. Sometimes they even demanded more from the people in terms of revenue than what was due. Even in case of Bandhan, there were instances when the *Mukhtar* demanded from the people more than what the Raja had fixed as his quota and thus he could retain the excess collection for himself.[174]

Raja Kirtichandra had appointed an *Uzir* for the general administration of Cachar valley. Govindachandra divided it into seven divisions, *viz*, Bikrampur, Arer-vitar, Dudpatil, Jaypur, Kalain, Sonai and Hailakandi, and appointed one *Uzir* each for all the divisions.[175] Krishnachandra had appointed some Brahmins as *deshamukya* for the judicial administration in selected areas.[176] These days there are almost in each *paragana* in Cachar some indigenous Bengalees Brahmin families whose hereditary title in *Deshamukhya*. Krishnachandra and Govindachandra also appointed some *Dalvi* to look after the internal deference of the state.[177] The institution of these offices resulted in the erosion of authority of the hitherto autonomous *Khels*.

Besides the heads of the *khels* and the state officials the individuals also came into prominence in some cases. The

172. Guha; pp. 121-3.
173. Sen; Nos, 106, 112-4.
174. Guha; p. 95.
175. *Ibid.*, p. 161.
176. *Ibid.*, pp. 176-7.
177. J.B. Bhattacharjee; N. 19.

twelve families of the Brahmins who came down to the plains from Maibong with the transfer of the capital settled in different parts of Cachar. They came to be known as *Aditya* and the heads of the original twelve families were collectively known as *Dwadash-aditya*. The traditions suggest that in all important matters of the state the Rajas consulted these *Adityas*.[178]

An important section of the Bengalee population in the valley belonged to the Nath (Yogi) community. Their number was also considerable, next perhaps only to the *palni*, they settled in several groups. Each group or village constituted a *Khanda-samaj* under a *murabbi* and a number of them constituted the *panch-samaj*, while a number of the latter constituted the *baro-samaj*. The Nath community in Cachar was divided into three such *bro-samaj*. In course of time, 16 of the Murabbis (possible one each from a panch samaj) emerged as the social leaders of the community. On their request the raja nominated these 16 to the *Ul*. This was perhaps the only instance of representation to the *ul* on the basis of community. However, these sixteen families came into prominence in the community and when Govindachandra distributed titles among the important, people in the state, the heads of these sixteen families also received such titles. The members of the whole Nath community in Cachar used to honour the heads of these families with pan (betel-nut and leaf) and pon (coin), and through them the control of the Raja extended over the whole community.[179]

The process of social stratification was also noticed among the *Dehan* of Koch who constituted for sometimes the ruling race in Cachar valley till succeeded by the *Dimasas*. The head of the *Dehan* society was called *senapati*, and the community had eighteen branches on the basis of hereditary functions. Besides the royal family, ministers, army etc., there were *Daloiv* (spiritual guide) dar (temple assistant) *purkait* (writer) singadar (flute man) *Kumarlaskar* (manufacturer of arms) *sonapatra* (goldsmith) *barpatra* (silver trader) etc.[180]

178. Guha, p. 95.
179. *Ibid*., pp. 196-8.
180. *Ibid*., pp. 34-5.

The example can also be given of another important community called *Hidla*. During one of his pilgrimages Krishnachandra brought in a few families from the valley of the river *Sitala* (sitalakha) and engaged them as *Devagrihi* (temple assistants) since they were considered to be of pure race and did similar work earlier. From *Sitala*/Sitla they came to be known as *Hidla* after Cachar Bengalees fashion of aspiring. They were perhaps originally of non-Bengalee origin, but gradually got totally assimilated in the Bengali society. In course of time, their population also increased and the different families came to be known as *Daloi, Badlai, Barkatir, Pani-katir, Majumdar, Deuri, Sarlaskar, Barbhuya, Kabibhuiya,* etc.[181]

Sometimes the individuals also by virtue of the wealth they possessed came to hold important positions in the society. The example can be given of Jumai Khan who identified an aguru forest in Berenga and with permission of Rajaj Lakshmichandra laid a settlement there, profitably carried on the *aguru* trade and emerged as an wealthy person. His son, Gulu Mian ingeirted the property and the business of his father, and helped Gambhir Singh in usurping the authority from Govindachandra. As a reward, Gambhir Singh gave him the title of *Nawab* and authorised him to fine and punish the criminals. He was entitled to a portion of the money collected as fine towards his honororium and the rest found way to the treasury.[182]

Only the Raja and the members of the royal family in Cachar were entitled to ride on horse or use pallanquin. A commoner could not use *Khesin* (blanket) gold or silver bangles and white umbrella.[183] Only the *Dhehans* enjoyed these special privileges and their *Senapati* could enter the royal courtyard in pallanquin.[184] An interesting incident occurred during the reign of Krishnachandra when his brother,

181. *Ibid,*. pp. 113-9.
182 *Ibid.*, pp. 139-40.
183 *Ibid.*, p. 132
184. Gait; p. 303; FPP, 14 May 1832, No. 101.

Govindachandra was the *juwaraj.* Marjit Singh, a fugitive prince of Manipur, entered Cachar on a horse's back, but on Govindachandra's order the watchmen confined the horse. When Marjit learnt the reason for the confinement he felt insulted and left for Burma. The aftermath of this incident was more unfortunate since with the help of the Burmese Marjit Singh captured power in Manipur and forced Govindachandra to escape from Cachar.[185]

These privileges were, however subsequently extended to the Choudhury, Majumdar and others who received such titles from Govindachandra by virtue of their wealth and position and on payments. In the *Farman* that Govindachandra issued to the title-holders the right to use blanket, gold or silver bangles, white umbrellas horse, pallanquin etc. were mentioned.[186] The title-holders on the other hand since then ruthlessly enforced the restrictions on others. Many stories about it are still current.[187]

Governing Factors

The transformation of the *Dimasa* political system from its indigenous tribal formation to a monarchical state was reached mainly through syncretic adoption of the symbols of Hinduism by bringing the tribes within the broad Hindu-based civilisation of Aryan Indians generated through the

---

185. Guha; p. 137.
186. *Ibid.*, pp. 178-9.
187. Once a farmer was passing through a village with his newly married wife who had used a golden nose-ring (*nath*). The information at once reached the *choudhury* of the area who immediately sent his guards and the ring was removed. In case one belonging to a lower caste had put on shoes, he was made to put on the shoes as garland before the public. In case of unauthorised horse-riding, the rider was made to sit on the back of the running horse from the opposite. The Choudhuries and other title holders thus commanded tremendous local influence that before long corrupted into oppressive conduct. But by virtue of their own position they were entitled to the privilege. Both in the hills and in the plains, as a matter of fact, there emerged a powerful nobility to look after themselves and the interest of the Raja.
Ibid., p. 132.

Bengal plains. The brahminical myths gave the ruling tribal clan a divine descent which added status and respectibility to the leadership of the tribal pattern and strengthened its base to integrate not only the cognate clans and ordering tribes but also the culturally and technologically more advanced Bengalees, universalising, in the process, their *"Kachai Kali"* cult through *Satka cult* of the Hindus and offering in return, the Brahmins, settled in and around the capital, a dominating position in regulating the state affairs by manipulating the court politics.

The process of state formation reached its crucial stage in Maigong, and at a time when in whole of the north-eastern region of India similar development took place; viz. Cooch Behar, Assam, Jayantia, Manipur and Tripuram, due mainly to the induction of a confronting situation inspired by the *Ahom* expansionism with superior military skill. The *Dimasas* had passed through initial experiments in state building earlier in the Brahmaputra valley and the archaeolgical evidence testifies the formative experiences at Dimapur where considerable Bengali influence has been noticed. The emergent leadership was legitimised through the Brahmins and its authority was further strengthened in the war path when the masses looked upon the Raja as the protection of their persons and the means of production.

The erstwhile valley landers resorted to both shifting and terrace cultivation circumstanced by the eco-system of the area under control which provided the appropriate techno-economic base for the generation of surplus. The control retained over the Kapili-Dayung-Dhansiri valleys in spite of the prolonged *Ahom* pressure in the west and the integration of the fertile Cachar plains in the south strengthened their economic base, and the state gradually attained absolute control over the forest and mineral resources and the brisk trade that passed through the tract. A firm and systematic control was maintained over the instruments of power through formal organisation of administration.

The use of Bengali language in administration and the patronage extended to Bengali literature served as an effective instrument in consolidating control over the more populous and revenue paying section of the state's population. The *Kshatriya* status gained in the caste Hindu society by the ruling clan and the tribal aristocracy was fruther legitimised by the adoption of this language. The state also provided elaborate institutional arrangements for the preservation of the tribal indentities in a multi-racial population structure within the state and at the same time took care to protect the revenue paying Bangalee subjects from interference of the court by drawing their own kinerds in the vital wings of the state structure. By his original tribal identity and the adopted Hindu-Bengali identity the reigning monarch could strike a balance between the contrasts in population composition located in isolated ecological settings. The stratification and the hierarchical social structure generated through Brahminical Hindu influences, drew sustenance for the state from indigenous ethnic traditions.

The *Dimasa* state in its final form was in fact built on the ruins of a number of formations in the areas that its bounds ultimately covered. The *Dimasas* themselves had passed through different stages of development and polity formation in Assam Valley, Dimapur and finally at Maibong by which time the Brahminical influences accelerated the process of social stratification and augmented the vested interests of the chief through a recognition of his status as the legitimate ruler of the people. In Cachar Valley, which ultimately became the core area of the state, a number of principalities and even states had emerged and declined by the time the *Dimasas* integrated the area into their own. The Tripuris ruled there till sixteenth century to be succeeded by the *Dehan* (Koch) principality petty principalities around the Dehan territory though sometimes independently and indifferently or, on occasions, in league or alliance with each other including the *Dehan* state. These traditions could be utilised by the *Dimasa* ruler.

The transition of the *Dimasa* society from a homogenous tribal structure to a system of stratified caste-type social groupings was indeed crucial in the process of state formation. The desintegration of the clan structure form purely genealogical groups into groups of socio-professional types, amounting to the rise of certain clans with a privileged social status accelerated the process of social differentiation and formation of a hierarchy. The stratification was marked by the rise of the clans of nobles and aristocrats, and those among them related to the Raja became more eminent. The continual war situation enabled the clans whose headmen enjoyed command of the military forces to claim higher status. The royal and noble clans in due course assumed *khastriya* status of the Hindu social order, when the Brahmins authenticated the divine descent of the Raja. The formation of the agriculturists, artisans and other professional clans resulted in further stratification and a distance between the higher and lower clans corresponding generally to the caste-order in Hindu society. The authority of the Raja over socially and economically unequal groups found sanction in his divine descent. The rude nature of punishment prescribed for various offences and the support of the bureaucracy in implementing these strengthened the autocratic rule, while his populist posture as the protector of the people and their religion ruled out descent in the hey days of the *Raj*.

The income of the state was guaranteed by the system of regular taxation of land and houses, trade and market and even fines. The commoners clans were required to render offerent types of services to the court, and every village or clan had to supply a certain number of labour at regular intervals. The private lands assigned to the members of the royal family and high officials including their *jhum* lands, had to be tilled by the specific clans. The agricultural surplus and market linkage influenced the early state formation, resulting in centralisation and sub-ethnic groupings.

The professional specialisation, uneven development, and emergence of an elitist state accelerated the process of social stratification and the growth of a hierarchical social organisation; but these status could not be equated with classes as the social linkages continued and the membership of a strata was determined by birth as in preclass/pre–capitalistic society rather than by relation to means of production as in class industrial societies. The *Dimasa* state was constituted by a system of village communities wherein the mutual relations corresponded to the pattern of disintegrating clan system, and the unity was only by the force of military power rather than any organic economic tie or economic predominance of the higher social groups. The progress of social stratification and increase in the number of socially differentiated groups till eighteenth century could mature further towards the formation of an early class society in appropriate conditions but the further evolutions of the social groups and their developments into classes was arrested by the decline of the state in the beginning of the nineteenth century. By the time the economy of the region had been monetized by British colonialism, the *Dimasa* state had already found a place in history.

5

NAYANKARA SYSTEM AND THE STATE IN MEDIEVAL TELINGANA

I. Laxmi

THE main purpose of this paper is to draw the attention of scholars to a region and period which offers wide variety of information for better understanding of medieval Indian state and society.[1]

So far the studies on early Indian history have been made viewing only the sources from comparatively developed zones such as Gangetic basin and in South Tamilnadu excluding the generalisation to the longer areas, while recognising the regional variations. None of them are

---

1. In the recent past histories have significantly contributed to the characterisation of Medieval Indian social formation. R.S. Sharma regarded it as feudal in Western European sense of the term. R.S. Sharma; *Indian Fudalism*, Delhi, 1965. See also *"How feudal was Indian feudalism"*, by the same author in *Journal of Peasant Studies*, Vol.8, No.3. April 1981. Harbans Mukhia elaborately emphasized the existence of free peasant production. Terry Byres and Harbans Mukhia *Feudalism and Non-European Societies*, London 1985.

   However, all these discussions concern widely with the developments in Medieval north Indian while for south India, it is Burton Stein who rejected the applicability of feudalism to Medieval south Indian society and offered an alternate theory 'segmentary state' applying it to chola and of Vijayanagar states. But B.D. Chattopadhyaya, R.N. Nandi, Noboro Karashima and D.N. Jha questioned the viability of this theory primarily because the concept is related to pre-state society and the source also does not subscribe to this idea. However, the entire debate led to the growth of very significant literature on the subject and raised

(Contd. to next page)

extended to the Andhra region in general and to Telangana region in particular. However, the need for region wise studies has been emphasized[2] in order to come to general as well as specific understanding of our history.

The political and socio-economic developments in South India between 10th and 14th centuries exhibit quite interesting traits which need to be studied thoroughly to understand the nature of the state. On the political scene there appeared regional linguistic dynasties like the *Hoyasala* (in Karnataka), the *Kakatiyas* (in Andhra), the *Pandyas* (in further South) and the *Yadavas* (in Maharashtra). The rise of these dynasties does not just imply only the shift in the political authority but is significant in many respects as the sources testify to number of socio-economic developments during the period.

The rise of these states signifies the shift in nuclear areas from plain fertile regions to high and thickly forested earlier peripheral regions which account for a number of developments. Growth of population, development of technology and growing importance of trade are considered to be some of the factors that contributed to the colonization of the high lands and establishment of new states. Such a shift led to the

---

(Contd. from previous page)

very important questions which are being examined by various scholars. Burton Stein; *"The Segmentary state in South Indian History"*, in edited volume by Richard G. Fox; *Realm and Region in Traditional India*, New Delhi 1977. *Peasant state and society in Medieval South India* (by same author) Oxford 1990. See also R.N. Nandi; *"Feudalisation of the state in Medieval South India"*, *Social Science probings*, Vol. I, No. 1, 1984. D.N. Jha; *"Validity of the Brahmana peasant Alliance and the Segmentary State in Early Medieval south India"*, *Social Science Probings*, Vol. I, No. 2, June 1984, pp. 270-96. B.D. Chattopadhyaya;" *Political process and structures of polity in early medieval India problems of perspective"*, Presidential Address (Ancient India Section) *Indian History Congress* 44th session, Burdwan, 1983.

N. Narashima; *South Indian History and Society, studies from Inscriptions A.D. 850-1800* Oxford 1984. Idem, *"Nayaka Rule in North and South Arcot Districts in South India during sixteenth century" Acta Asiatica Tokyo*, 1985, pp. 1-26. I Thank Prof. B.D. Chattopadhyaya of centre for Historical studies, Jawaharlal Nehru University, New Delhi for his valuable suggestion while writing this paper.

2. Romila Thaper; *"Interpreting Regional History"* in *Ancient Indian Social History*.

conclusion that nuclearity of region is finally a historical chronological and not purely geographical category and the nuclearity of the region is related to how historical factors converge on it and not merely to its resource potential.[3] However, the quest for the control of fertile areas continued to manifest in the continuous campaigns the rulers undertook.

For the present study we choose the Telingana region which has been termed as central Deccan. This region for the first time became the seat of political power during twelfth century.

The Telingana region is thickly forested hilly region and as such the lands were 'Second choice' lands which did not attract early settlements. However, by the time of the *Kakatiyas* i.e. by eleventh century the region provided sufficient basis for the emergence of political authority from within while next state which had its centre in Telingana was *Qutub Shahi* state.[4]

The shift (from geographically dominant regions) proved successful with the growing importance of trade in the society.[5] Nevertheless, agrarian source potential being primary factor also developed by extending the area under cultivation through deforestation and by providing artificial irrigation.[6]

The growth of settlements and the establishment of political authority in Telingana was a slow and gradual process spreading roughly to three centuries i.e. from ninth to twelfth.[7]

The studies made on South India have opened a variety of relatively new methods particularly relating to the nature of political authority, the question of land ownership and irrigation, social stratification and the role of the temple both

---

3.. B.D. Chattopadhyaya. *Op. Cit.*
4. J.F. Richards considers the Qutub Shah as 'conquest state' *Idem; Mughal Administration in Golconda*, Oxford, 1975.
5. I. Lakshmi,"*Economy, Society and Polity in Telingama-11th ot 14th Century A.D.*", unpublished Ph.D., Thesis, JNU, 1987.
6. *Ibid.*
7. A.B. Mukharjee, "*Succession of landscapes in Telingana Reddi Villages*", *Indian Geographical Journal*, Vol. XXXIX, 1962.

as a ritual and social centre. This paper, is linked only to the first aspect i.e. to the nature of political authority.

The *Kakatiya* Polity presents very interesting mechanism of appropriating the locally dominant elements into the political structure. In the early stages of its emergence it largely relied on local chiefs who equally contributed to the rise of the dynasty. After the establishment of the dynastic control over the region the rulers in order to consolidate their power in a changing socio-economic order had to think of an alternative to loose feudatory system which resulted in the introduction on *Nayankara* system. The system worked as an integrating mechanism of potential groups. It is this theme which is elaborated.

The early political structure was loosely knitted with the feudatory chiefs[8] called as *samanthas* and *mandalikas* who were enjoying semi-independence if not total independence by maintaining their own courts and army. They were functioning as *Senapatis* in the King's army.[9] Among the *Samanthas*, depending upon their strength and relation with the ruler, there was gradation.[10] The royal authority needed the support of the feudatory chiefs whose allegiance, however, was not reliable. Moreover, due to the perceptible changes in the socio-economic and political conditions by thirteenth century the later members of the ruling dynasty needed to introduce a new system of administration by replacing the hereditary chiefs by appointed chiefs i.e. the *Nayankara* system.

---

8. In the inscriptions of the feudatory chiefs, they are mentioned as *Samanthas, Dandanayakas and Mahamandaleswaras* whereas the rulers of the Kakatiya dynasty are mentioned as *Mahasamanthas* and *Mahamandaleswara* without (assuming) any exalted titles. *Inscriptions of Andhra Pradesh* (hereafter referred as *IAP*), Warangal Nos. 27, 29, 48 and 64; *Corpus of Inscriptions in the Telingana Districts of the Nizam's Dominions* (hereafter referred to as *Corpus*) II, Nos. 50, 51 and 52.
9. *IAP* Wgl. No.17.
10. Members of the Natavadi family are mentioned as *Mahamandaleswara* while the members of the rest of the feudatory families such as the Recherba, Viriyala and Malyala families are mentioned as *Mandaliks, dandadhipas* and *Senapatis. Ibid.*, Nos. 17, 27, 29 Etc. *Corpus* II, Nos. 50, 51 and 52.

The *Nayankara* system which was the most dominant aspect of the Vijayanagara rule had its emergence in the Kakatiya period. However, it is not the present concern to deal with the linkages between the *Nayankara* system of the Kakatiyas and that of the Vijayanagar rule. The system seems to have assumed all feudal traits by the Vijayanagara period. Noboru Karashima[11] while studying the *Nayaka* rule in North and South Arcot district of Tamilnadu came to the conclusion of existence of feudals systems as the *nayakas* assumed all rights concerning the management of production in local areas and were functioning as feudal lords.

The present paper thus attempts to trace the emergence of the system basing upon the changes that have occurred in the society. Various factors had necessitated the introduction of the new system in the polity of the period.

About 30 inscriptions form Telingana region are examined for the present study. This selection has been made with the view that the political changes are easily perceptible in the core region of the kingdom and throughout the Kakatiya rule the region was under their control.

The early inscriptions mentioning the term *nayaka* (the leader generally used for the head of the tribe) from Telingana indicate their presence at village level. An undated epigraph[12] belonging to the time of Eastern Chalukya king Bhima from Koravi states that neither *nayaka* nor *Kampu* (cultivator) who join the enemy king should live in the village. Both the *nayakas* and *kampus* were the *sudras*. The former were the warrior group while the latter were the cultivators as the agrarian settlements of the region were dominated by *Sudra*

---

11. He states that " The image of the *nayakas* of the 16th century in North and South Arcot districts, as a group who were granted the territory and the legitimacy of their rule by the king on the one hand, and who strengthened their power through the accumulation of certain rights concerning the management of production in local areas on the other may allow us to regard these *nayakas* as feudal lords and interpret the 16th century in south India as the period when feudal relations developed to a certain degree at least in one region". Noboru Karashima, *Op. Cit.*, p. 26.
12. *IAP*, Wgl. No. 6.

warrior/ cultivator goups.[13] Another early reference[14] to the *nayaka* indicates that they were among village functionaries. The inscription dated A.D. 1108 from Bairanipalli, Jangaon Taluk mentions twelve *nayakas* among the King Vikramaditya VI's subordinates. In the particular instance the *dandanayaka,* the two *karanams,* and the twelve *nayakas* of Bhuvanagiri were entrusted with the execution of the Charity to Vittakulathilaka Jinalaya of Bekkallu, made by certain Birama Reddy and Punni Reddy. Taking the order given in the inscription the hierarchy can be established. The *nayakas* were of the lower rank than the Karanam and above him was the *dandanayaka.* It is interesting to note that these people were entrusted with the maintenance of the thalavritti, the gift meant for white-washing and repairing of the temple and for feeding the monks. The purpose of the gift was to be met from the incomes which were to be derived from the *mavina ratana* (water drawing device), 20 *marturus* (a measure of land) of karaṃba land irrigated by the *yerayamayya nakera,* 2 *marturus* of wet land, irrigated in the months of *kartika* and *vaisakha,* a coconut grove on the bank of the palavalige *tore* (stream), and one oil mill etc. The inclusion of twelve *nayakas* in the maintenance of the grant consisting land and oil mill is indicative of their position in the village making them indispensible party. Another inscription[15] dated A.D. 1116 states that certain pila Bace Nayakundu made a gift of 2 *rukas siddhayamu* (tax on shops). He was the subordinate of Kanduri Gokarna Maharaja (a Teluguchoda ruler). It is thus obvious that the *nayakas* were initially military professionals functioning as tax collectors. A careful examination of the later epigraphs reveals that by twelfth century *nayakas* were associated with the royal authority in different capacities as *tantrapalas, mahapradhanis*[16] etc.

By the middle of twelfth century we get references to the

---

13. A.B. Mukherjee; *Op. Cit.*
14. *Corpus,* III, mn. 11.
15. *Ibid.,* Km.
16. *Ibid., Ng. 1 and Corpus II, No. 33.*

individual *nayakas* claiming *samantha* status.[17] These inscriptions suggest that the *nayakas* who constituted *sudra* warrior group could rise to hold different positions in the political structure of the period, which they must have got as a reward for their loyalty and achievement.

By thirteenth century we find the *nayakas* being associated with the *nayankaras,* which were also called as *sthalas,* indicating the emergence of the regularised order of *nayankara* system. The period falls under the rule of Rudramadevi and Prataparudra respectively. By late thirteenth century the system had crystalized into an alternative to the feudatory chieftaincies.

It is only the literary sources[18] belonging to a little later period that we get details about the introduction of *nayanakara* system ascribing it to the ruler prataparudra. Accordingly there were about seventy five *nayakas* each assigned with a *nayankara* and had to maintain the stipulated army.

One obvious factor which necessitated the introduction of the system was war. During the rule of Rudramadevi and Prataparudra very few feudatory chiefs obliged the authority of the rulers.[19]

Apart from internal revolts they had to face constant battles with the Yadavas and the pandyas. In addition to these the Delhi Sultanate from the times of Allaudin Khalji made the Kakatiyas face a number of invasions from north. The ruler Prataparudra had to purchase peace a number of times by

---

17. An Inscription date 1120 from Matedu states the donor of the grant as *"Samastha Prassasti Sahitam bunasriman Mahasamantha Vema cholo,* Boddama Nayaka who was the *Bamtu* (Soldier/loyal servant) of *Mahamandaleswara* Prolaraja of the kakatiya dynasty who in turn was the subordinate of western Chalukya ruler Thirbuavana Malladeva.*IAP*, Wgl. No. 24. Another record from Alugadapa dated A.D. 1207 mentions the donor Gundapanayaka as Vadhuri *Puravaradhiswara Corpus,* III, Ng. 1.
18. *Ekamranatha Prataparudra Charitramu* (Ed.) C.V. Ramachandra Rao, Hyderabad,1984; *Kase Sarvappa, Sidheswara Charitmmu* (Ed.) K. Lakshmi Ranjanam, Hyderabad. 1960 *Velargolivari Vamsavali,* Compiled by N. Venkataramanayya, Madras.
19. See N. Venkataramanayya and M. Somasekhara Sarma," *The Kakatiyas of Warangal"* in G. Yazdani, (Ed.). *The Early History of the Deccan,* parts VII-XI, Oxford, 1982 (first published in 1960) pp. 620-65.

paying large quantities of gold, elephants etc.[20] The mobilization of indispensable resources during wars necessitated administerial changes which the conclusion of peace consolidated. There was increase in the number of taxes imposed on people. An effecitve collection of taxes could be ensured only through appointed officials. It led the state to endow itself with a permanent bureaucratic infrastructure leading to new kind of relationship with the subjects.

The military assistance which the feudatories provided to the king lacked the certainty of assistance and the amount of army maintained by them varied from feudatory to feudatory, and lacked uniformity in recruitment and training. These Kakatiyas against their opponents particularly the Delhi Sultanate. Taking into account the political situation where the feudatories started disobeying the ruler, as he was facing external threats, the rulers had to ensure services through an alternative. Under such need the *nayankara* system was found as a new means of ensuring services. Though the creation of the system can be explained as being necessitated by war but it was only an immediate factor. It is from thirteenth century that we get references to the gifts made by the mercantile and artisan groups, indicating the rise in their economic and social status. These sections were organised into guilds (or corporate bodies) which regulated their economic activity and social organisation of these groups coincides with the introduction of the *nayankara* system. The state in order to get substantial incomes from these goups needed a direct control over such areas, through direct administration. *Nayankara* system can be stated as a step oriented towards that end. It was an attempt of centralization of administrative and military functions. Thus the inscriptions, recording the grants of *astadasa praja*[21] in which merchants and artisans weare pot come from the *nayankara* areas which were also called the *sthalas* constituting a number of villages. The head quarters of *nayankaras* were

20. K. Satyanarayana; *A study of History and Culture of Andhras* PPH, New Delhi, 1975.
21. *Corpus*, II.

towns. Apart from the grants of *astadasa praja,* grants of merchant organisations too came from *nayankara* areas. Towns being the headquarters generally the concentration of the *nayaka* will be on the town activity. It is trade factor which primarily distinguishes a town from rural settlement. The Manur *sthala* which was a *nayankara* constituted twelve villages and the epigraph[22] from the place record the gifts of *astadasa praja.* Likewise Magatala *sthala* was the *nayankara* of *Maharayagajasahini, swamidrohara ganda* Gundayanayaka.[23] The Tekumbedla *sthala* was the *nayamakaramu* of *Mahapradhanin puravari* (superintendent of revenues) ·*mahadeva nayankulu.*[24] These references also indicate that the *nayakas* not only administered the *nayankaras* but also held other posts such as *puravari* and *Mahapradhani.* From the titles which the *nayakas* held it is apparent that there was gradation among the *nayakas. Nayankara* system can be seen as some what nearer to the order of knigththood in Europe. The *nayakas* had all the potential to develop as feudal lords as the inscriptions mention that some *nayakas* were the samanthas perhaps they were already feudal lords while some others give details where all members of a family being *nayakas* while possessing all esalted titles the *nayakas* mention themselves to be *'bamitu'* i.e. the loyal subordinate. All the inscriptions of *nayakas* suggest that the *nayakas* become an order by themselves. This later could have become a caste. In one instance they are referred to be belonging to *Pulindavamsa* and to have been created to protect the four castes.

Regarding the recruitment of *nayakas* N. Venkataramanayya[25] states that "they belonged to no single community in particular but were recruited from all classes...." At another place[26] he mentions that all the ministers and other

22. *Ibid.*, III, Ng. 1.
23. *Ibid.*
24. *Op. Cit.*, p. 642.
25. *Ibid.*, p. 662.
26. *Op. Cit.*, p. 195.

officials held commissions in the army in virtue of the *nayankara* system". While P.V.P. Sastry[27] states all the erstwhile *samanthas* under this system were entrusted with the responsibility of maintaining compulsorily some army for the service of the king in times of war." We cannot agree with the latter's view as the whole system was oriented towards replacing the old order of feudatories. The mention of 'lenkas' the body guards of the ruler[28] as *nayakas* in some inscriptions suggest that these most loyal and trusted persons were also appointed as the *nayakas*. This way various officials in royal service were also rewarded with the *nayankaras*. Thus the recruitment into the *nayankara* system was a reward to those who were loyal to the ruler. The *Nayankaras* in Rayalaseema area were created with a different function. Primarily in Rayalaseema area the *nayakas* had to concentrate on extension of agriculture.

The whole kingdom was not of course under the *nayakas* as there were still some feudatory chiefs who obliged the political authority of the Kakatiyas. Thus it was period of both vassal and subject as the system was an attempt to establish direct link between the ruler and the ruled through an appointed chief.

Finally the study of the emergence of *nayankara* system would enable us to understand the attempts of political authority to centralize the political power by integrating the rising social goups. These attempts point further to the changing political structure during the period. The changes in social order with the rise of artisan and merchantile communities necessitated the changes in political structure.

---

27. The Lembas were slaves who had entered into a covenant with their lord to devote themselves exclusively to his service. They took an oath (basa) to look on their lord as their *guru* and deity in this world and the next, to have no regard either for their own property or for their lives in furtherance of his interests, to stand by him in the hour of danger, to fight his battles, either to perish with him in the clash of arms or to kill themselves if they should chance to survive". N. Venkataramanayya; *Op. Cit.*, p. 680.
28. K. Satyanarayana; *Op. Cit.*

Though the attempt was made to bureaucratic the system, the direct control over people, the power to collect taxes, and feasibility of the system to become hereditary, finally resulted in feudalisation of the system.

INDEX

A

Abbasiad Caliph of Egypt, 29
Abmanyu, 30
Adil Shah, 42
Aditya, 95, 113
Aditya, Krishnaram, 105
Ahoms, 80, 81, 83, 86, 88
Akbar, 2, 10, 52
Alam, Muzaffar, 48, 49
Alaud-din Pora, 21
Albuquerque, Afonso de, 32, 41
Aligarh School, 45
Ali Hamadani, 12, 18, 19
Allaudin Khalji, 126
Alu Raje, 94
Amir-ul-Muminin, 29
Angami-Dimasa relations, 89
Angami Naga, 88, 102
Arer vitar, 112
Arimatta, 80
Assam, 87, 116
Asuritikar, 87
Athar Ali, M., 45
Aurangzeb, 55, 60, 64
Avtar Batia, 30
Awad, 48
Azam, Muhammad, 54

B

Bachaspati, Bhubaneswar, 92
Bahadur, Said Khan, 54, 55
Bahadur Shah, 42
Bairanipalli, 124
Banaras, 103
Baqir, Azam Khan Mir Muhammad, 64
Barak Valley, 80, 95, 106
Barman, Anantaram, 99
Barman, Chandra Mohan, 99
Barman, Maniram, 99
Bayly, C.A., 46
Bengali literature, 98, 99, 116-17
Bhattacharjee, J.B., 71
Bhima, 123
Bhim Raja (Bhimadarpanarayana), 89
Bhim Singha, 95
Bhuyan, S.K., 79
Bihari Mal, 55, 56
Bijbehare, 12
Bikrampur, 112
Biradarpanarayana, 88
Brahmanbra, 93
Brahma Purana, 93
Brahminical Hinduism, 86, 98, 103
Byquiyin, Coje, 38

C

Cabral, Pedro Alvares, 34, 38, 41
Cachar, 72, 79, 80, 84, 87-90
Caharir Niam, 92
Cannanore, 41
Claessen, Henry J.M., 75-77
Chand, Rai-Sabha, 56, 65
Chelah, Yosuf, 64
Chnilaraj, 86

Cooch Behar, 116
Correa, Aires, 35

D

Darya Khan, 30
Das, Raj Kashi, 65
Delhi, 63, 66
Dersongpha, 82
Dhamadi, Haor, 93
Dhanamanik, 87
Dharmadhyakshya, 83
Dharmapur, 95
Diger Kacharis, 89
Dimapur, 80-82, 86, 92, 116
Dimarua, 86
Dimasa State in Medieval North East India, 71, 119
- Categories of state, 71-72
- Conceptual frame of, 73-74
- Decline of, 162-04
- Dimasa case, 78-80
- Early state model, 75-78
- Governing factors of, 72, 115-19
- State formation, 80-102
- Early phase, 80-82
- Final phase, 94-102, 117
- Intermediate phase, 82-94
- State structure of, 104-15, 117-18
- Aditya in, 113
- Administration of, 106
- Bengalee affairs, 106-07
- Functional authority of, 105
- Hindu symbol and legends, 105
- Judicial powers, 109-10
- *Khel*, 107-08, 111
- *Khes*, 110-11
- Members of court, 111-12
- Mukhtar as official of, 108
- Privileges to, 114-15
- Revenue, 108-09, 118
- Secular attitude, 110
- Social stratification, 113-14
- Uzir apointment, 112

Dipalpur, 63, 66
Dossuki, A.E.H., 8
Dudpatil, 112

E

East India Co., 102
Eminabad, 64
Endle, S., 79
Engels, Friedrich, 71

F

Fazal, Abul, 52, 57, 68
Fiqh, 12
Firuz, 12
Fisher, Thomas, 84

G

Gait, 81
Gambhir Singh, 105, 114
Ganapati, Gaurak, 30
Ghatokkachanarayana, 84
Gilani, Sheikh Moosvi, 57
Gilani, Syed Abdul Razzaq, 55
Gopi Chander, 95
Gopi Chander Panchali, 89, 95
Gopichandra, 95, 102
Gopi, Malik, 42
Govindachandranayana, 84, 94, 96-105, 108, 111-12, 114, 115
Gujarat, 64
Gulu Mian, 114
Gundayanayaka, 128

H

Habib, Irfan, 45
Hacengsa vangsaja, 85
Hoglong, 75
Haider, 11
Hailakandi, 112
Hangloo, R.L., 5
Hanifia doctrine, 8

Haranya-garve ceremony, 98
Hardwar, 103
Harischandra, 95
Harischandra II, 95, 97
Harishchandranarayana, 85
Harmba-rajya, 84, 85
Hassan Simnani, 11
Herabheswara, 85
Herambha, 85
Hidla, 114
Hoyasala, 120
Hunter, 97
Huton, J.H., 89

I

Indrapratapnarayana, 87
Indravallabhanarayana, 85
Inscription from Bairanipalli Jangaon Taluk, 125
Ishaq Mukarram Khan Mir, 55
Islam, 6

J

Jahangir, 64
Jalandhar, 63, 66
Jamil Hafiz, 30
Jamul-ud-din Alai, 12
Jasanarayana, 87
Jasrat Khokhar, 31
Jayadhraj Singha, 88
Jayantia, 66, 87, 116
Jaypur, 112
Jen Kins, 89
Jonaraja, 25, 27, 30

K

Kachai Kati, 83
Kachari, 75, 76, 81
Kakar, Dilawar Khan, 53
Kakatiyas, 120-22
Katain, 112
Kalicharan, 90, 91
Kalicharan Upakhyam, 90
Kamal, 12
Kamarpara, 93
Kamrup, 80, 86
Kanchain, 95
Kanch-Dammara, 30
Kanduri Gokarna Maharaja, 125
Kangra, 58, 59, 63, 65
Kapil, 89
Kapil-Dayaung-Dhansiri, 86
Karpura-Bhatta, 30
Kashmir, 6, 7
Khail, Akta, 52
Khalifas, 19
Khan, Afzal, 63, 65
Khan, Ali Mardan, 56, 62
Khan, Amanat, 56
Khan, Dianat, 56, 65
Khan, Firoz Rustom, 64
Khan, Jumai, 114
Khan, Khanazad, 59
Khan, Lashkar, 54
Khan, Mir, 59
Khan, Mir Ahmad, 64
Khan, Mubariz, 63
Khan, Mukarram, 55, 60
Khan, Najabat, 62
Khan, Sardar, 63
Khanqas, 6, 13, 27
Khaspur, 96, 97
Khorapna, 82
Khourpara, 12
Khunkara, 82
Khutba, 8
Kirtichandra, 90, 112
Kirtichandranarayana, 92, 94
Kirtipur, 87
Kishtwar, 31
Koch state, 94, 95
Koravi states, 123
Kirshnachandra, 92, 96, 103, 107, 111, 112, 115
Kulgam Pargana, 12

Kumararpara, 93

L

Ladakh, 31
Lahore, 53-56, 66
Lakhi Jangal, 62, 63, 65, 66
Lakshimakas, 9
Lakshmichandra, 95, 114
Lakshminarayana, 111
Laskar, Maniram, 92
Laukika calendar, 8
Laxmi I., 119

M

Madrasas, 12
Mahabharata, 84
Mailbong, 82, 85, 87, 88, 92, 94, 95, 116
Main, Khwaja, 53
Majumdar of Bikrampura, 98
Malacca, 42
Malik Autar Chand, 30
Malik Ayyaz of Diu, 42, 43
Manipur, 86, 90, 116
Mansur Bin Mohammad, 30
Manuel, Dom, 34
Marakkar, Cherina, 40
Marakkar, Mamale, 40
Maretina, Sofia A., 75, 77
Marjit Singh, 115
Mathew, K.S., 33
Maymame, 36
Mayuradhraja, 92
Medieval Indian State, 1-4
  Accounts of, 1
  Foundations of, 1
  Historical process of, 1
  Legitimize functioning of, 3-4
  Mughal rule, 2-3
  Overlapping historical circumstances, 2
  Social transformation of, 1
Meghanarayana, 85, 87
Miku, 88
Mir Jumalah, 88
Mir Mohammad Hamadani, 21
Mir Qaiser, 27
Mir Sayyid Fakhru-ud-din, 12
Mir Sayyid Kazim, 12
Mir Sayyid Mohammad Abdullah, 12
Mir Sayyid Mohammad Qurashi, 12
Mir Sayyid Rukum-ud-din, 12
Moamaric rebels, 88
Muazzam, Muhammad, 54, 63
Mughal rule, 2-3
Mughal state in 17th century Punjab, 45-69
  Bureaucracy of, 50-51
  Bureaucratic hierarchy of, 52-53
  Economic change, 46-47
  Faujdar office, 57-65
  Faujdar suppression, 63
  Faujdar transfer, 62
  Financial administration, 56-57
  Formation of local socio-political elites, 47-48
  Fragmentation of Mughal empire, 49-50
  Gardens by, 51
  Intra-regional transfers, 54-55
  Jajmani Jagir, 48-49
  Knowledge of regional peculiarities, 55-56
  Mansabdars, 57, 66-68
  Mughal crisis in, 48
  Mughal system, 45, 48
  Periodical transfers of officials, 51-54
  Political actions of, 52
  Political integration in, 49
  Qiladars, 61
  Territorial jurisdictions, 63-64, 67

Transfer principles, 68-69
Muizz-ud-din, 63
Mulla Ahmad Kashmiri, 30
Mulla Kabir Kashmiri, 30
Mulla Nadri, 30
Mulla Qazi Khan, 30
Multan, 52-53, 63, 66

N

Nagam paragana, 12
Naidkhai, 12
Nagshbandi, 17
Naradiya Rasamitra, 93
Nath community, 113
Naushera, 31
Nayaka rule, 124
Nayakundu, 125
Nayankara System and State in Medieval Telingana, 119-29
Administration system of, 122-24, 128
Dominant aspect of Vijayanagara, 124
Forested hilly region, 122
Inscriptions in, 124-26
Kakatiya polity, 125
Literary sources of, 126
Military assistance with feudatories to, 127-28
Nayakas associated with nayankaras, 126
Nayakas recruitment, 128-29
Political and socio-economic developments, 121, 129
Political authority, 122-23, 128
Political structure of, 128
Settlement growth, 122
Trade in, 122
Wars of, 126-27
Nirbhoyanarayana, 82, 84, 94
Nizam Shah of Ahmadnagar, 43
Noboru Kareshima, 124
North Cachar Hills, 89
Nothsoma, 30
Nora, Joaode, 39
Nowgong, 86, 89, 95
Nurul Husan, S., 45

P

Pandyas, 121
Pemberton, 89
Perlin, Frank, 47, 48, 50
Portuguese trade in sixteenth century India, 33-44
Attitude of rules with, 40
Bijapur, Ahmednagar and Gujarat trade with, 42-43
Defeated at Chaul, 37
Equality of status, 38
Exchange of commodities, 33-34
Fight between Zamorin and Portuguese, 37
King of Cannanore trade with, 40-41
Loss to commercial prosperity, 36-37
Portuguese factory at Calicut, 34-35
Portuguese wanted special treatment, 36
Quilon trade with, 41
Trade facility to, 38-40
Vijayanagar rulers relations with, 43-44
Zamorin of Calicut contact with, 34-35
Zamorin treatment to Portuguese, 35
Prataparudra, 126
Pratapgarh, 87
Pratapnarayana, 85, 87
Punjab, 45-69

Q

Qadri, 17
Quilon, 41
Quli, Murshid, 56, 62
Quran Hadith, 12
Quranic obligation, 16
Qutub Shahi, 122

R

Radcliffe-Brown, A.R., 71
Rajanak, 30
Raja Rani Chandraporara, 94
Rajouri, 31
Rajrup, 62
Ramachandi, 83, 111
Ramachandranarayana, 90
Ramraja of Vijayanagar, 43
Ranachandi, 85, 87, 103, 104
Raya, Krishna Deva, 43
Rayalaseema, 129
Razzaq, Abdul, 55
Rechards, J.F., 46
Reddy, Birama, 125
Reddy, Punni, 125
Rudramadevi, 126
Rudra Singh, 81
Rudra Singha, 88
Rungreng, 90
Rupya Bhatta, 30

S

Sadiya, 80
Saifu-ud-din, 27
Sailkot, 64
Sakti, 33
Sastry, P.V.P., 129
Satrudaman, 87
Sayyids, 5-32
Sayyid Mak, 29
Seikh-nosor-ud-din, 30
Sempora, 12
Shafi, Muhammad, 56
Shahi Khan, 28
Shahjahan, 52
Shahmir Sultan, 5-32
  Administrative system, 30
  Army of, 9-10, 29
  Endowments to Sayyids, 13-14, 21-22
  Hindu converts, 22, 27
  Hindus persecution, 26
  Islam issue, 6-8
  Islamization promotion, 23-24
  Relations with neighbouring regions, 31
  Religion and state relations, 14-17
  Sayyids as political ideologues, 21
  Sayyids as social bans, 17-18
  Sayyids as Sufis, 10-11
  Sayyids authority, 22-24
  Sayyids interference in affairs, 20-21
  Social order and authority of, 7-8
  Stability of, 32
  Suherwardia order, 18-19
  Sultans submissin to Sayyids, 26-27
  Ulama, 7-8
Shams-ud-din Shahmir, 8-11
Shariat, 16, 22
Shikoh, Dara, 55, 57
Shriya Bhatta, 30
Shuja, Najabat Khan Mirza, 54
Sialkot, 64
Siddiqi, N.A., 45
Sikander, 21-23, 25-26
Sinha, 30
Sirhind, 63, 65, 66
Sita, Kantha, 30
Siva, 85
Siva Bhatta, 30

Skalnik, Peter, 76, 77
Snan Mandir, 97
Sonai, 112
Sonapur, 89
Srinagar, 12
Srivara, 30
Stein, Burton, 47
Suradarpa, 93
Suradarpanarayana, 92, 94
Suraj Mal, 62
Surma Valley, 89
Suharwardiya, 17, 118
Sultanpur, 66
Sylhet, 87, 89, 92

T

Taj-ud-din bin Sayyid Hassan, 12
Tamradhrajanarayana, 92
Tarkhan, Ghazi Beg, 53
Tekumbedla, 128
Telingana, 119
Tihara, 63
Tilka Acharya, 30
Todar Mal, 63, 65-67
Tripura, 80, 86, 90, 116
Tripura Buranji, 89
Tulaman, 102
Tularam, 96, 111
Turani, Qulij Khan, 53-55

U

Uditnarayana, 87
Umma, 79
Upper Assam, 80

V

Vaisnavism, 97
Vasco de Gama, 34-36
Venkataramanayya, N., 128
Vijayanagar, 43, 44, 124
Vikramaditya VI, 125
Viradarpanarayana, 85
Visnugarh, 111
Vittakulathilaka Jinalaya of Bekkallu, 125

Y

Yadavas, 111
Yasanarayana, 85
Yazdgird, 8
Yodha Bhatta, 30
Yousuf Khan, 28

Z

Zain-ul-Abidin, 10, 28, 29, 31, 32
Zamorin of Calicut, 34-38
Zimmis, 29
Zutshi, 26